The
Bosom
Serpent

Harold
Schechter

The Bosom Serpent

Folklore and Popular Art

University of Iowa Press
Iowa City

ψ

University of Iowa Press, Iowa City 52242
Copyright © 1988 by the University of Iowa
All rights reserved
Printed in the United States of America
First edition, 1988

Book and jacket design by Richard Hendel
Typesetting by G&S Typesetters, Inc., Austin, Texas
Printing and binding by BookCrafters, Chelsea, Michigan

Library of Congress Cataloging-in-Publication Data

Schechter, Harold.
  The bosom serpent.

  Bibliography: p.
  Includes index.
  1. Urban folklore—United States.   2. United
States—Popular culture.   3. Legends—United States.
I. Title.
GR105.S34   1988   398'.0973   87-23780
ISBN 0-87745-193-1

For Leslie Fiedler

Contents

Preface

       Sometime in 1980, a year or so after the birth of our first child, my wife and I were told the following story. According to our neighbor, who'd heard this from a friend who knew the couple in question, two teenage parents were driving down the Long Island Expressway on a muggy summer day when their Chevy overheated. They pulled onto the shoulder, popped open the hood, and set their five-month-old daughter, still securely strapped into her portable safety seat, onto the roof of the car, where she could enjoy whatever fresh air was available. Before very long, a quarrel broke out between the young parents, and they were still going at it even after the engine had cooled and they were back on the road. Indeed, they were halfway to the Midtown Tunnel before they stopped shouting. Only then did they notice that their baby daughter was uncharacteristically quiet—in fact, their baby daughter wasn't in the car.

The story had an upbeat ending. As it happened, the baby's safety seat had slid off the roof the moment the car began to move. Landing upright on the shoulder, it was immediately spotted by a passing motorist, who retrieved the child and was waiting with her by the roadside when her frantic young parents came zooming back onto the scene. Even so, my wife and I were seriously unsettled by this tale. For people who had recently become parents themselves, the hair-raising experience of the heedless young couple was a potent reminder of our own daunting new responsibilities. I recall that we indulged in a bit of armchair analysis, speculating about the subconscious motives of the two teenagers, whose behavior, we concluded, betrayed a great deal of ambivalence toward their five-month-old charge.

I felt slightly abashed, therefore, when, several years later, I was reading Jan Harold Brunvand's *The Choking Doberman* and discovered that my psychologizing had been expended on a pair of completely fictitious characters—that the story I'd accepted as fact was, in reality, a type of contemporary tall tale that folklorists know as an "urban legend." In retrospect, it's clear that this wildly improbable yet strangely compelling little anecdote (which Brunvand labels "The Baby on the Roof") consists entirely of traditional folk-tale elements—shockingly bad parents, an abandoned babe, a miraculous salvation—recast in strictly contemporary terms. And, like any good folk story, this one manages to play on very primal emotions while reflecting the preoccupations and anxieties of a particular time and place—in this case, the worries, insecurities, forbidden wishes and concomitant guilt millions of young(ish) Americans were experiencing for the first time in the early 1980s when, having delayed marriage and parenthood until their mid-thirties, the members of the so-called baby boom generation, my wife and myself included, were busily creating a new mini–baby boom of their own.

What brings this story to mind right now is its appearance—seven years after I first heard it from my next-door neighbor—in a recent film comedy, Joel and Ethan Coen's live-action Looney Tune *Raising Arizona*. At one point in this rollicking redneck farce, a pair of bumbling fugitives kidnap an infant, then accidentally lose him by leaving him on the roof of their getaway car during a typically inept gas-station holdup. Encountering the story this time, however, I felt neither the chill that went through me when I heard it first nor the sense of having been gulled that I experienced when I came upon it in Brunvand's collection. What I felt this time was pure gratification.

It's always nice to have your insights validated, and the appearance of "The Baby on the Roof" in a 1987 slapstick movie is simply the latest confirmation of this book's basic thesis—that in our high-tech time and consumerist culture, the traditional folk narratives that have provided pleasure to human beings since storytelling began are transmitted to us largely through the popular media.

This book grows out of the countless arguments (some more polite than others) I've found myself engaged in throughout most of my adult and all of my professional life. Because my taste in narrative entertainment tends to differ in significant ways from that of my colleagues and friends, I've frequently had to defend myself against charges of crassness, infantilism, or willful eccentricity (if not active perversity). It's not that I spend all of my spare time at the drive-in. As the following chapters will, I trust, make clear, my tastes in literature and film are, I believe, fairly catholic. But it is certainly true that my fondness for things like splatter films, supermarket tabloids, and E.C. horror comics is genuine, deep, and abiding. In an effort to explain (to myself as much as anyone, I suppose) exactly what there is about American pop culture, particularly in its trashier manifestations, that makes it so appealing to me, I have undertaken this study—and one of the nicest things about having completed it is that presumably I won't have to spend so much of my time having the same arguments anymore. From now on, when anyone asks me, "Why do you *like* that stuff?" I can simply refer him or her to my book.

Since I like to believe (pretentious though this may sound) that I take Emerson's injunctions to writers and thinkers seriously, I've tried to make this a very personal book. The works I deal with are those that have exerted the strongest and most sustained grip on my imagination; indeed, some of them have remained powerfully alive inside my head since childhood. But (since my tastes are not quite as aberrant as they are sometimes perceived) they are also representative works both of American pop art and of the particular genres they belong to. Moreover, since all folk stories (as Robert Darnton makes clear in his splendid study, *The Great Cat Massacre*) function as "social documents" as well as archetypal fantasies, the texts I treat in the following pages say a good deal about the cultural obsessions and conditions of the post–World War II period, an era that corresponds (not coincidentally) to the decades of my own life.

Among those friends and colleagues who have encouraged, challenged, or simply humored me for years and, in so doing, have prompted or compelled me to put my ideas into order, I'd especially like to thank Morris Dickstein, Tom Frosch, Don McQuade, Ann Davison, Ray Browne, Leslie Brill, Bruce Kawin, and Jerry Herron. I am also grateful to the Research Foundation of the City University of New York for its consistent and generous support of my work.

My greatest debt, however, is owed to Leslie Fiedler, whose teaching and writing have immeasurably deepened my understanding of the relationship between our culture's official myths and secret dreams and of the sense in which any successful criticism of pop entertainment has to be a form of pop entertainment itself. In *What Was Literature?* Fiedler writes that "it is a major mystery of my career that I have come to be regarded as a 'seminal' . . . critic even though almost every one of my books has been more scorned than praised in the academic and literary reviews." The solution to that mystery, I believe, can be located in Emerson's "The American Scholar," which portrays an intellectual ideal that Fiedler comes closer to fulfilling than any contemporary critic I know:

> If a single man plant himself indomitably on his instincts, and there abide, the huge world will come round to him.

The
Bosom
Serpent

1 | The Bosom Serpent

Folklore and Popular Art

The folklore and fairy tales of yesterday take up where the mythology of the ancients left off. They are, as Freud said, the run-down mythology of former times. Today, a new form has been found. It is represented by the movies, the "funnies" or comic strips, and most recently by the new art of television.
—Martin Grotjahn,
  Beyond Laughter

The central problem of popular culture criticism—how to say meaningful things about, for instance, a *Teen Titans* comic book without making preposterous claims for it—is complicated by the fact that few people who practice such criticism seem to know just what popular art is, what distinguishes it from (as well as connects it to) serious or "high" art. The reason for this state of affairs, as Leslie Fiedler suggested in *What Was Literature?* (and I suspect that the unusually savage reviews the book received were at least partly the result of his having suggested this), is simply that most popular culture critics are academics—more often than not ones with a training in literary analysis—and therefore tend to respond to "mass art" in one of two ways:

1. Some of these critics entirely ignore the bulk of popular art, being baffled (if not actively threatened) by any imaginative work they cannot dazzlingly dissect through the application of their highly developed exegetical skills. I've noticed this phenomenon especially among academics who teach and write about film, and experienced a direct demonstration of it not too long ago when a colleague and I had a dispute over Stanley Kubrick's *The Shining,* a self-proclaimed "masterpiece of modern horror" which I found pretentious and only mildly and intermittently disquieting but which he loved. Why? Because of its cinematography, editing, "sly comedy," and thematic complexity, all of which he was quite expert at discussing in the most subtle and even elegant terms. In short, he was one of many film specialists I've known who appreciate pop art insofar as it approximates high art; that is, to the degree that it lends itself to the kind of intellectual analysis, the formal and thematic explication, they are used to performing with such virtuosity on literary texts. As for truly *pop* horror movies, movies which are aesthetically crude, thematically null, often brutally scary, and which attract far larger (if less discriminating) audiences than the Kubrick film ever did (*Friday the 13th, Maniac,*

The Evil Dead, and *Amityville 3-D* are a few examples), my friend regarded them with good-natured contempt, even though he hadn't seen any of them or even heard of one or two.

2. The other group of popular culture critics consists of those who really do relish things like low-grade horror movies, tacky TV sitcoms, and *Conan the Barbarian* comic books but, for various reasons, are compelled to rationalize their tastes in the highly sophisticated (and often ludicrously inappropriate) terms of their favorite methodologies. These are the critics who fill up the pages of certain academic journals and the panels of scholarly conferences with meticulously researched studies of Jane Austen's influence on "I Love Lucy," the stylistic complexities of "Beetle Bailey," and the allegorical meanings of "Star Trek"—studies whose high-flown language and weighty tone are so utterly at variance with the unabashed schlockiness, the essential (and I use that word in both its senses) vulgarity of the subject matter, that it's hard to believe they weren't written in the same parodic spirit as Frederick Crews' *The Pooh Perplex,* that classic of mock-Milnean scholarship which should have made such academic pretentiousness at least a little harder to perpetrate.

The temptation (or compulsion) to talk about pop art in these intellectualized terms is undoubtedly a form of defensiveness. Often, careerist considerations are involved: the effort to justify one's interests to skeptical, if not openly hostile, colleagues (many of whom regard popular culture studies as part of a pervasive breakdown of academic values that they trace back to the 1960s) by demonstrating that a *Scrooge McDuck* comic book can yield as many meanings as *Paradise Lost* (well, almost) when approached with the proper critical tools. I suspect, however, that an even more important factor is the need for these critics to rationalize their fondness for midnight movies and Saturday morning cartoon shows to *themselves*—to reassure themselves that it's okay to take pleasure in (as well as devote their professional attention to) such lowly fare.

In the end, critics of this kind, who (like the authors of air-line menus) describe the most undistinguished offerings in the fanciest possible terms, seem to know just as little about the true nature of popular art as those colleagues of theirs who remain cheerfully oblivious to nine-tenths of it. It isn't simply that, for the most part, pop entertainment is so utterly unpretentious (the imaginative equivalent of fast food) but that the quality which people prize it for, which makes them such avid consumers, is one that is notoriously resistant to analysis by traditional criticism.

This is the quality that Stephen King, in the preface to his collection of magazine pieces *Night Shift*, identifies as "story value." "All my life as a writer," King tells us, "I have been committed to the idea that in fiction the story value holds dominance over every other facet of the writer's craft; characterization, theme, mood, none of these things is anything if the story is dull. And if the story holds you, all else can be forgiven."[1] But, of course, it is precisely characterization, theme, mood—along with style, tone, symbolism, and other technical and formal elements—that academic critics attach the most importance to, whereas they tend to regard the quality that King is talking about with either condescension or outright scorn, dismissing works in which a strong narrative is the predominant feature as mere "potboilers" or "page-turners" and the people who produce such works as, at best, "natural" (i.e., crude if effective) storytellers (unless, as occasionally happens, such a writer manages to make it into the pantheon, like James Fenimore Cooper, in which case he is promoted from "storyteller" to "mythopoeic artist"). King himself is perhaps the most notable contemporary example of a writer whose works are constantly denigrated by highbrow critics for their literary shortcomings (particularly their folksy, "let's-go-have-a-beer-and-talk" style, as one reviewer put it, acknowledging that he would "just as soon have a beer with [King] as read him").[2] Meanwhile, these same books are powerfully appealing to countless "average readers," who devour King's horror yarns by the multi-millions and couldn't care less about the quality of his prose.

Why critics should depreciate the very aspect of fiction that is the main source of pleasure for the vast majority of readers—indeed, that has nourished the human imagination since story-telling began—is an interesting question. Snobbery undoubtedly has something to do with it: the intelligentsia's ingrained and often automatic disdain of most things beloved by mass audiences (an attitude epitomized by several self-styled intellectuals I've known who take pride in their refusal to see any movie or read any book that achieves wide popularity—*E.T.*, for example, or *Love Story*). Other factors include self-interest—the unavoidable fact that academic critics, whether of literature or film, have a personal stake in convincing people (including themselves) that the value of any work is located precisely in those qualities that only an academic critic is equipped to shed light upon—as well as the fear of the nonrational, the discomfort many academics feel in the presence of stories that play on their emotions so brazenly. On the whole, academics tend to be a pretty controlled bunch and much prefer works which are intellectually challenging to melodramatic or sentimental stories which wring an emotional response out of readers (or viewers); that is, threaten at least a temporary loss of control.

I am not arguing, of course, that pop entertainments distinguished by a strong narrative line and little else in the way of psychological complexity, formal excellence, thematic significance, etc. are superior to the works preferred by the critical elite—that *Kiss Me Deadly* is a better book than *Middlemarch* because once you start a Mickey Spillane novel you just can't put it down. As a teacher of literature I am only too aware of the pervasive philistinism among "general readers" and movie-goers. If academics tend to look down their noses at the millions of "mass-cult" consumers who choke on anything less insubstantial and bland than a TV sitcom, the contempt flows freely in the other direction, too, so that the typical fan of "Love Boat," for instance, is likely to regard someone who admires *My Dinner with André* as part of a vast conspiracy of effete, pseudo-intellectuals who define art as anything that the ordinary person can't make head nor tail of.

At times it's tempting to reduce the difference between popular and high art to a fundamental split between "child" and "adult," as long as we understand those terms as metaphors for two different, though not necessarily incompatible, parts of the human personality that exist, in varying proportions, in most of us: the part that delights in pure fantasy and play, and the more "serious" (i.e., educated, discriminating) part that is capable of responding to the formal and intellectual qualities of art. In this respect, pop art can be regarded as "childlike," appealing, as the saying goes, to "the child in all of us"—though the problem here, of course, is that the label seems so inherently judgmental. As a result, even those who prize pop art's ability to keep them in touch with the "child" within—to nourish that unruly, unsocialized side of ourselves that we outgrow at our own risk—may be reluctant to call that quality by a name which would undoubtedly confirm the deepest prejudices of elitist critics who are only too ready to condemn all of pop art as immature, uncouth, and "regressive."

But this inner child is precisely that part of us which, like a toddler at bedtime, is highly susceptible to the enchantment of a beguiling or astonishing or swiftly paced tale, so that it is possible, I believe, to identify an imaginative work as popular (and here we come back to Stephen King's observation) by the emphasis it places on sheer narrative. Popular fiction (a category which includes comic books as well as such "post-Gutenberg"[3] forms as TV soap operas and most Hollywood movies) may therefore be defined as mass-produced art whose primary goal (whatever else it may achieve, intentionally or not, in terms of style or theme) is to reach out to (and into) the widest possible audience by telling a story that triggers a very basic and powerful emotional response: wonder or terror, laughter or tears, suspense or erotic arousal.

This definition, it seems to me, clears up some of the basic confusion that has always surrounded popular culture studies, particularly the problem I began by discussing: the general inability of critics to find cogent ways of distinguishing pop art from high. Efforts to define the former according to standards of popularity, for example (which might, on the face of it, seem logical), are inevitably frustrated by the awkward existence of legions of mass-market paperbacks and Grade-Z exploitation movies that are complete commercial failures—in short, that aren't popular at all. The issue, however, isn't the size of the audience that a particular work attracts but the nature of the material; that is, the extent to which it relies on pure story appeal to sell the product to the consumer.

More importantly, this definition makes it clear that any piece of criticism that evaluates a popular narrative—a Robert Ludlum thriller, say, or a movie like *Porky's* or *Flashdance*—according to criteria appropriated from traditional literary scholarship is inevitably going to make both the work and the critic look unnecessarily bad. The critic, by insisting so emphatically on the seriousness of his subject matter, is bound to come across as someone who protests a bit too much, while the work can only end up looking like decidedly second- (or third- or tenth-) rate art: skillfully constructed, perhaps, but completely devoid of "higher" value. ("Staggeringly inept on any human level," is the way Morris Dickstein puts it in an attack on *The Road Warrior*,[4] as though a stunning feat of storytelling were not in itself a significant human achievement.) By the same token, high art is apt to seem seriously deficient when measured against the standards by which the general public gauges the success of a movie or book. While a film by Eric Rohmer may offer pleasures that cannot be matched by *Rocky IV*, an exciting, action-packed plot isn't likely to be one of them—and the fan of Sly Stallone who finds himself sitting (no doubt against his will) through *My Night at Maud's* has some justification for feeling that he's watching a movie in which, as far as he's concerned, "nothing happens."

What all this suggests is that it may be time to start looking at pop art in a different light—not as a primitive, rudimentary form of "real art" (as though Harold Robbins, say, were a kind of literary Neanderthal on a ladder of aesthetic evolution whose highest rung is represented by the late novels of Henry James) but as part of an age-old tradition of popular or communal story-telling, a form of fiction which, in spite of superficial similarities to serious art (both *The Carpetbaggers* and *Wings of the Dove* have characters and plots and can be purchased in either clothbound or paperback editions), actually bears a much closer resemblance to folklore.

The relationship between folklore and popular art has been noted by a number of critics and scholars. In his classic 1934 essay "Style and Medium in the Motion Pictures," for example, Erwin Panofsky examines the "folkloristic" background of the movies and shows how, by appealing to the mass audience's taste for "sentiment, sensation, pornography, and crude humor," pop films continue to reflect a "folk-art mentality."[5] Leslie Fiedler, too, though he reserves the term "folk literature" for the story and song "of pre-literate society,"[6] clearly perceives an affinity between the two types of narrative, popular and folk. One of the defining characteristics of the former, he points out, is a certain anonymous quality that is also characteristic of folklore. Like fairy tales and legends, popular fiction is distinguished by a special kind of immortality: what remains alive is not the language of the original text or even the name of the creator but simply the story itself:

> As a matter of fact, one of the distinctions between popular and high literature can be made on the basis of this, as Edgar Allan Poe, in a review of James Fenimore Cooper,

pointed out. There is a certain kind of book, he wrote, which is forgotten though its author is remembered (High Literature); and there is a certain kind of book whose author is forgotten though the work is remembered. And it is indeed true, isn't it, that at the present moment there are far more people who can identify Hemingway than can identify Lt. Henry or Jake Barnes; while Sherlock Holmes is a familiar name to many people who have never heard of Conan Doyle. And the name of Tarzan is known to everyone in the world, including those who never heard of the name Edgar Rice Burroughs.[7]

Interestingly, Burroughs himself seems to have understood the anonymous nature of his art, proclaiming at the very start of *The Land that Time Forgot*, "Read page one and I will be forgotten," a striking confirmation of Poe's idea that, in the realm of pop literature, it is only the story that matters.[8]

On the whole, specialists in folklore have been somewhat more alert than pop culture critics to the connections between the two fields. Though certain folklorists, such as MacEdward Leach, condemn modern "mass culture" as completely destructive of "folk song and story,"[9] others recognize a more complex and vital interplay between traditional, oral legendary and the media. Writing in 1968, for example, German scholar Hermann Bausinger argued that industrialization has not meant "the end of . . . folk culture" but rather its "mutation and modification,"[10] a point of view shared by American folklorist Linda Dégh, who, in an influential 1971 essay, called on her colleagues to "expand their field of exploration . . . beyond the 'folk' level to identify their material as it blends into mass culture."[11]

Perhaps the most clear-sighted effort to pursue Dégh's suggestion is a 1976 study by Ronald L. Baker, "The Influence of Mass Culture on Modern Legends," which examines the reciprocal relationship of pop culture and folklore.[12] "On the one hand," Baker writes, "the products, institutions, and heroes of mass culture have had an enormous impact on the subject matter of contemporary legends," a phenomenon that can be seen in a wide range of "belief tales" from the so-called "Paul McCartney Death Rumor"[13] to such consumerist horror stories as the widely circulated report that Bubble Yum chewing gum is manufactured from spider's eggs or that a child actor in a popular TV commercial died by internal explosion after consuming a pack of Pop Rocks candy and then washing it down with a Coke.

On the other hand, Baker continues, pop fiction and music, motion pictures, television, radio, "and other mass media have engulfed and spread a number of legendary themes."[14] Although Baker himself provides only a few examples of this process (a radio version of "The Vanishing Hitchhiker" legend and a scene in a Doris Day movie based on the tale of the "Weekend Camper"), his point is supported by W. M. S. Russell, whose 1981 presidential address to the Folklore Society of London examines the "folktale background" of scores of science fiction novels, from H. G. Wells' *When the Sleeper Wakes* (a version of the "venerable motif of Magic Sleep Extending over Many Years") to Isaac Asimov's *Foundation* trilogy (a scientific elaboration of the Golem legend).[15]

Seeing popular art as a kind of mass-produced folklore—as the form of storytelling that has taken the place of traditional folk narrative in the technological world—makes it clear that, in general, the very phrase "popular art" is a serious misnomer, since art, the aesthetic, is as utterly irrelevant to the appeal or meaning of most movies, comic books, and TV shows as it is to the average Dead Baby Joke.[16] To be sure, even the most unassuming jokes and oral legends require a degree of artfulness in the telling. As eminent folklorist Jan Harold Brunvand points out, the best "performers" of such well-known urban legends as "The Cat in the Microwave" and "Alligators in the Sewers" employ "carefully orchestrated . . . gestures, eye movements, and vocal inflections." They do so, however, not for art's sake but for the sole purpose of getting their stories across more effectively, of making them, as Brunvand says, "dramatic, pointed, and suspenseful." [17] Certainly, the language of the following tale, a version of the widespread legend of "The Boyfriend's Death" collected from a University of Kansas freshman and presented by Brunvand as an example of a particularly skillful "folk narrative style," is completely nondescript and functional, simply a vehicle for conveying a shock:

> This happened just a few years ago out on the road that turns off 59 highway by the Holiday Inn. This couple were parked under a tree out on this road. Well, it got to be time for the girl to be back at the dorm, so she told her boyfriend that they should start back. But the car wouldn't start, so he told her to lock herself in the car and he would go down to the Holiday Inn and call for help. Well, he didn't come back and he didn't come back, and pretty soon she started hearing a scratching noise on the roof of the car. "Scratch, scratch . . . scratch, scratch." She got scareder and scareder, but he didn't come back. Finally, when it was almost daylight, some people came along and stopped and helped her out of the car, and she looked up and there was her boyfriend hanging from the tree, and his feet were scraping against the roof of the car. This is why the road is called "Hangman's Road." [18]

It is possible, of course, to make aesthetic judgments about even the schlockiest of popular works. Pop aficionados, from comic book collectors to splatter movie fans, tend to be every bit as discriminating (in their own way) as opera buffs. They regard certain works as major artistic achievements (e.g., *Uncle Scrooge* comic books drawn by Carl Barks or issues of *Creepy* magazine with cover illustrations by Frank Frazetta) and pub-lish scholarly pieces on the subtleties of *Blood Orgy of the She-Devils* in homemade "fanzines" like *Gore Gazette* and *Sleazoid Express.* In the end, however, amateur criticism of this variety seems just as misguided as the kind of pop culture criticism practiced by most academics. It's as though the defenders of pop can think of no other way of establishing its worth and sig-nificance than by making (largely untenable) claims for it as art.

The uncomfortable fact is, however, that the great majority of popular works are unredeemed by anything resembling aes-thetic quality. And those exceptional commercial authors or filmmakers or comic book illustrators whose works *do* possess "higher" values—psychological complexity, thematic richness, stylistic grace—are precisely those who come to be recognized as serious artists working within popular forms, so that, for ex-ample, Ursula K. Le Guin's transition from pulp novelist to *New Yorker* writer seems not only natural but inevitable, as does the decision by curators of the Whitney Museum of American Art to mount a 1983 exhibit featuring R. Crumb's cartoons.

The question for academic critics of popular culture, however, is not how to deal with Le Guin's *The Left Hand of Darkness* (a science fiction novel every bit as complex and well written as any of the novels of, say, John Cheever) but what to do with a movie like *They Saved Hitler's Brain* other than dismissing it as a "camp classic" or a serious contender for the title of "Worst Movie Ever Made." And one answer is to look at it as folklore; indeed, as a specifically modern variant, transmitted tech-nologically instead of orally and reflecting our ongoing obses-sion with Hitler, of the motif of the "Severed-Yet-Living Head," a "widespread folk belief" found "from China to Peru, from the Celtic North to the Americas, Africa, and the Antipodes."[19]

Such movies are quite similar to those lurid, sensationalistic tabloids that fill the supermarket magazine racks and seem like fifty-page illustrations of P. T. Barnum's famous dictum. With their blaring come-ons for items like Magical Zodiac Bracelets and Do-It-Yourself Cosmic Dust ("Use it to bring good fortune, punish evildoers, and heal the sick!"), these publications are virtual anthologies of age-old folk themes reincarnated in contemporary terms. The January 3, 1983, issue of the *Weekly World News*, for instance, features headline articles such as "MAN BLOWS UP ON OPERATING TABLE," "RADIO-ACTIVE CAVES RELIEVE ARTHRITIS PAIN," and "DE-VOTED HUSBAND RETURNS FROM THE GRAVE WITH A ROSE FOR BELOVED WIFE," each one a precise analogue of widely known folktales cataloged in Ernest Baughman's standard *Type and Motif-Index*.[20]

One of the virtues of the folklore approach to popular culture is that it recognizes the irreducible value of pop art without making unconvincing attempts to redeem it from vulgarity. After all, it seems self-evident that stories which have survived for so long and continue to exert such a powerful appeal must possess some important meaning for the human imagination.

The folktale essence of pop entertainments that seem strictly contemporary in terms of subject matter and storytelling technique can be seen in the 1983 movie *War Games*, a flashy, fast-paced thriller that turned out to be one of the year's biggest blockbusters. At a glance, the primary appeal of this film—about a young computer "whiz" who nearly sets off World War III by tapping into our national defense system with his Apple IIe—would seem to be its extreme topicality. A closer look, however, reveals that the movie is really a high-tech retelling of the traditional story of the "Sorcerer's Apprentice,"[21] in which a different sort of "wiz"—a novice wizard—tampers with powers that are beyond his control and causes a catastrophe from which he is saved by the timely appearance of his master, a role played in *War Games* by master programmer Professor Falken, who originally devised the defense system at NORAD and who comes to the hero's—and the world's—rescue at the movie's end. In short, what we have in *War Games* is an age-old folk narrative decked out in the most up-to-the-minute guise, and the tremendous commercial success of the film attests to the timeless and apparently intrinsic appeal of such tales.

War Games also illustrates an important psychological function of folklore as it manifests itself in the popular arts. By taking two current issues that are sources of deep anxiety and bewilderment for millions of people—the so-called computer revolution and the renewed threat of nuclear war—and transforming them into an archetypal narrative, the movie offers us a way of making sense of developments that seem too overwhelming to grasp. In effect, the film reassures us that the crisis we are currently living through, far from being unprecedented, is really a perennial human experience—"the same old story" in updated form. Furthermore, it offers us the comfort of tried-and-true folk wisdom, suggesting that catastrophe can be averted if we will simply heed the very commonsensical message of the tale; that is, refrain from meddling with forces that we have not yet learned to master.

The built-in appeal of folk legends has been exploited by a large number of filmmakers, many of whom deliberately incorporate folk themes into their work or even build entire movies around them. Though this strategy can be found throughout the history of film—the "Severed-Yet-Living Head," for instance, is a favorite (indeed, almost an obsessive) motif in the work of Georges Méliès, and Howard Hawks' 1941 *Ball of Fire*, about a gangster's moll (Barbara Stanwyck) who moves in with a houseful of adorably eccentric professors (Gary Cooper among them), is simply a screwball-comedy remake of "Snow White and the Seven Dwarves"—it seems particularly prevalent in contemporary movies aimed at teenage audiences. Folklorist Larry Danielson has amply documented how extensively drive-in horror films like *Fraternity Night, When a Stranger Calls, Silent Night, Evil Night,* and *Halloween* draw on modern urban legends. *Halloween* alone relies so heavily on various belief tales, including the ones known as "The Assailant in the Backseat," "The Boyfriend's Death," "The Roommate's Death," and "The Endangered Babysitter,"[22] that Danielson describes the movie as a "composite of themes and motifs familiar to any folklorist who has paid attention to . . . oral horror stories," as well as a striking illustration of the relationship between "urban legend and modern film."[23]

Other such illustrations abound. Indeed, it is possible to find recent cinematic variants of almost every folktale collected in Jan Harold Brunvand's *The Vanishing Hitchhiker*, the first of his entertaining studies of modern urban legends. In the 1983 hit *National Lampoon's Vacation*, for example, an elderly character called Aunt Enid (Imogene Coca) inconveniently expires while driving cross-country with her nephew-in-law (Chevy Chase) and his family. Stuck in the middle of nowhere and disinclined to share a car seat with a corpse, Chase wraps Aunt Enid in a tarp, straps her to the luggage rack, proceeds to her son's house in Phoenix, and deposits her on his doorstep. Except for its resolution, this episode is a precise cinematic analogue of the widely distributed legend known as "The Runaway Grandmother" (most versions end with an added bit of black humor: having stopped for a bite to eat before disposing of the body, the family emerges from the restaurant to find that their car has been stolen from the parking lot).[24] Another popular urban folktale, "Alligators in the Sewer" (which, as Brunvand shows, has been in circulation since at least the 1930s),[25] is the clear inspiration for *Alligator*, a 1976 *Jaws*-style horror movie which concerns a twenty-five-foot renegade reptile on the loose below the streets of a small midwestern town and which well may be, as screenwriter John Sayles claims with justifiable pride, the greatest giant alligator movie ever made.

A film called *Hilary's Blues*, produced in 1973 but unreleased until a decade later, contains a scene in which (to quote

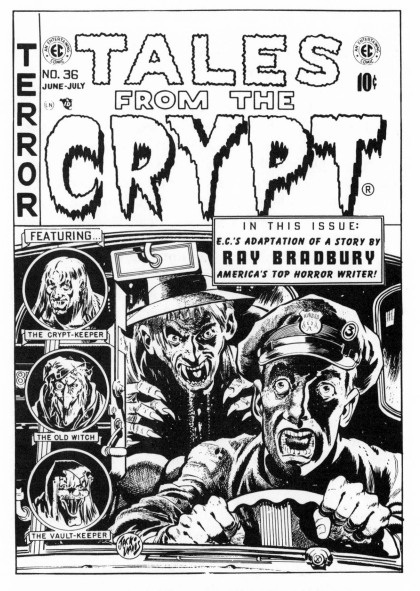

*"The Assailant in the Backseat." Cover art from the E.C. horror
comic* Tales from the Crypt *36 (1953). © 1987 by William Gaines.
Reprinted by permission.*

Janet Maslin's review in the *New York Times*) "an acquaintance of [the protagonist] takes LSD and then confuses her baby with the Thanksgiving turkey,"[26] an episode obviously derived from the modern American legend of "The Hippie Babysitter," the "usual versions" of which, writes Brunvand, involve "a somewhat freaky-looking babysitter" who "gets high on marijuana (or LSD, or even Scotch) and cooks 'the turkey,' that is, the baby, in the oven."[27] The prologue to 1983's *Twilight Zone* movie—a self-contained little chiller in which the driver of a car (Albert Brooks) gets a nasty surprise when his amiable passenger (Dan Ackroyd) turns out to be a vampire—is a variant of a very durable legend that Brunvand labels "The Roadside Ghost."[28] And the innumerable teenage slash-'em-ups, in which young, sexually active couples are set upon by knife- (or ax- or chainsaw-) wielding psychos (*The Burning, Madman, Prom Night, My Bloody Valentine*, etc.), are simply drive-in versions of the many legends about the Lover's-Lane Maniac ("Cropsey" and the "Hook-man" are two of the better-known avatars of this mythic figure) that are an apparently universal feature of teenage American folklore.[29]

It's worth noting that, though horror movies of this type have been widely denounced as symptoms of rampant misogyny, they are really (as Alan Dundes has shown in an illuminating study of their folktale analogues) projections of adolescent anxieties common to both sexes. And to the degree that the victims *are* more frequently females, the movies (again, like the folktales) reflect the traditional warnings that young women receive about the dangers of putting themselves in sexually vulnerable situations and their consequent fear that, given the right set of circumstances (e.g., a parked car in a remote area at night), "Even nice boys . . . sometimes act like sex maniacs."[30]

This is not to say, of course, that it is only popular art which has close ties to folk belief. On the contrary, folklore has served as an inexhaustible source of inspiration (and material) for serious artists throughout the ages, and scholarly journals are filled with articles examining the folklore borrowings of writers from Chaucer to Thomas Pynchon, from the *Beowulf* poet to Joyce Carol Oates. The difference between the serious and the popular artist in relation to folklore is that, almost invariably, the former will utilize a folk motif as a way of achieving some larger (frequently thematic) end. As H. R. Ellis Davidson says in an essay on "Folklore and Literature," the "method of the creative writer . . . who makes use of folk beliefs is not to declare his position either for or against them but to use them to suggest various meanings."[31] What we tend to get in popular works, on the other hand, is pure folklore cast, to be sure, in contemporary terms and communicated through sophisticated, technological means, but essentially unmodified. In short, whereas serious art transforms the raw material of folk literature, popular art simply transmits it. For the most part, popular narratives are nothing more (or less) than folk stories: the same spooky or amusing or salacious or cautionary tales that people have always wanted, or needed, to hear.

A look at how a common (albeit bizarre) folk belief is embodied in two radically different works—Hawthorne's short story "Egotism, or, the Bosom Serpent" and Ridley Scott's 1979 science fiction/horror movie *Alien*—will help illustrate my point. The belief in question is cataloged in Baughman's *Type and Motif-Index* under the heading "Snake Enticed Out of Man's Stomach," and variants of it (as Brunvand among others points out) are well known in this country from New England to Texas.[32] Indeed, Hawthorne himself notes at the start of his story that "the physical fact [i.e., a serpent inhabiting a man's body], to which it is here attempted to give a moral signification, has been known to occur in more than one instance,"[33] and a number of scholars have attempted to locate the immediate source of Hawthorne's tale in various newspaper accounts of this "phenomenon" that appeared in the early nineteenth century.[34]

Although specific details vary from version to version, the

*"Death from Swallowing a Mouse." This 1876 engraving from
the London tabloid the* Illustrated Police News *is an example of
a "creature-in-the-body" contamination legend, a variant of the
Bosom Serpent motif.*

basic outline of the legend—which, as Robert D. Arner has
shown, is at least "as old as the sixteenth century"[35]—is as follows: Through some unfortunate circumstance or act of carelessness (eating watercress contaminated with snake semen,
inadvertently swallowing a frog's egg while swimming in a lake,
sleeping open-mouthed beside a pond or stream), a snake (or
similar creature, such as a frog, salamander, or "spring lizard")
is accidently ingested by, or grows inside the body of, the un-
lucky individual, where it remains until it is expelled or in some
way lured out of the victim's body (usually by enticing it with

food). The following account, one of scores that have been reported by folklorists, will serve as a representative example:

> Early in 1916 this story was being much talked about . . .
> A woman had lately swallowed a frog, or a frog's egg, which
> lived and grew inside her. She was taken to Stroud Hospital [in Gloucestershire, England]. And they tried to open
> her, but they couldn't open her, because it moved about.
> And she was in such agony that she asked them to give her
> poison and put her out of her misery. So they wrote the
> King to ask if they might poison her, and the King wrote
> back to say No, they mustn't. Then the doctor put a piece of
> cheese on her tongue, and the frog smelt it and came up,
> but as it came up it choked her. And they do say that frog
> weighed half a pound. [36]

This widespread belief tale is at the center of "Egotism, or, the Bosom Serpent," though, as Hawthorne makes clear in his footnote, his interest is not in the story itself but rather in its "moral signification." And, indeed, "Egotism" turns out to be one of the author's more labored attempts to extract a larger meaning from, or impose one on, some remarkable (though supposedly authentic) "fact." The story concerns a young man named Roderick Elliston who, after perversely abandoning his wife, Rosina ("the ideal of gentle womanhood" [p. 172]), suffers a profound physical and emotional "blight" apparently produced by an "odious reptile" (p. 174) that has somehow infiltrated his breast. Again and again (and again) Hawthorne informs us that the protagonist's condition is a "symbol of monstrous egotism" (p. 176), an emblem of "diseased self-contemplation" (p. 183), a "type of each man's fatal error, or hoarded sin, or unquiet conscience" (p. 179). Endowed by his affliction with a heightened "perception of frailty, error, and vice" (p. 176), Roderick takes to roaming through the city streets, laying bare the hypocrisies of his neighbors through a form of what Hawthorne describes as "light satire":

> One day he encountered an ambitious statesman, and gravely inquired after the welfare of his boa constrictor; for of that species, Roderick affirmed, this gentleman's serpent must needs be, since its appetite was enormous enough to devour the whole country and Constitution. At another time, he stopped a close-fisted old fellow, of great wealth, but who skulked about the city in the guise of a scarecrow, with a patched blue surtout, brown hat, and moldy boots, scraping pence together, and picking up rusty nails. Pretending to look earnestly at this respectable person's stomach, Roderick assured him that his snake was a copperhead, and had been generated by the immense quantities of that base metal with which he daily defiled his fingers. . . . Observing a married couple whose domestic troubles were a matter of notoriety, he condoled with both on having mutually taken a house adder to their bosoms. (pp. 177–178)

"Egotism, or, the Bosom Serpent" is certainly not without interest, particularly to a student of Hawthorne; dealing as it does with issues like isolation, obsession, intellectual pride, hidden sin, and the redemptive power of a good woman's love, the story is a compendium of Hawthorne's central concerns. Yet it never comes alive as a piece of fiction. Part of the problem is simply the uncharacteristic clumsiness of the writing. Roderick's "light satire" is, in fact, embarrassingly heavy-handed, while some of the supposedly unsettling descriptions of his "snaky nature" (p. 172) verge on the inadvertently comic. The image of Roderick "undulat[ing] along the pavement in a curved line" (p. 171), for example, is more suggestive of a rhumba dancer than a man possessed by a "bosom fiend." More damaging, however, is the fact that the high "moral signification" which Hawthorne attaches to the "foolish belief"[37] is ultimately less interesting, or resonant, than the belief itself. By straining so hard after allegory, Hawthorne drains the central fantasy of its dreamlike (or, more properly, nightmarish) energies and reduces a potent legend to a flat and mechanical sermon.

By contrast, the hit movie *Alien*, for all its visual sophistication (its stylish cinematography and flashy effects), bears a much closer resemblance to the unadorned folktale. Whereas the motif of the "bosom serpent" serves Hawthorne as a "point of departure" for his thematic concerns, a "ready-made moral symbol,"[38] the space-age variant we get in *Alien* is devoid of intellectual pretension. Like the traditional oral versions that have been popular for hundreds of years, its only purpose is to produce an emotional response: shock, revulsion, morbid fascination.

The motif appears near the start of the film, when a three-man search party, exploring a grim, alien planet, comes upon a derelict spaceship, the bowels of which are filled with hundreds of football-size eggs. As one of the explorers (John Hurt) bends close to an egg to examine it, it suddenly springs open and a slimy, long-tailed creature—resembling an extraterrestrial horseshoe crab, minus the shell—leaps up and attaches itself to Hurt's face. (This first, rudimentary form of the film's constantly metamorphosing monster was nicknamed the "face-hugger" by its creators.) Sometime later, this parasitical creature shrivels up and dies, but not before depositing an egg in the body of its victim, so that, when Hurt sits down for a meal after regaining consciousness, a ferocious, eel-like creature abruptly bursts from his chest in an explosion of blood and bone.

Clearly, every element of this horrific episode is precisely analogous to the folk motif of the "bosom serpent": the initial act of carelessness, the implantation of the egg inside the person's body, the ultimate emergence of the monster when a plate of food is set before its human host. Whether or not the makers of *Alien* were conscious of these connections is, finally, irrelevant, as is the fact that the existence of this particular variant depends, not on the narrative skills of an amateur storyteller, but on state-of-the-art cinematic technology and a multimillion-dollar budget. For what we have in *Alien* is, in essence, a futuristic folktale: a centuries-old story retold in terms that are consonant with the obsessions of our age. It can even be argued that in attempting less, thematically, than Hawthorne's story does, *Alien* ends up by accomplishing more, since, instead of imposing a single, limited meaning on the motif of the "bosom serpent," the movie (like so many folktales) allows it to speak its own obscure but compelling dream-language. And if we are so inclined, we can even engage in a bit of allegorical interpretation of our own, seeing, in the memorable image of the "face-hugger," an emblem of those qualities shared by folklore and the popular arts: an apparent simplicity of form combined with the ability to grip us in surprisingly powerful, even irresistible ways.

2 | The Bloody Chamber

Terror Films, Fairy Tales, and Taboo

I had planned to depart as soon as I'd seen enough to write a clever pan, but we stayed to the bitter and bloody end—committed participants in the quintessentially American ritual of the drive-in and the junk movie. Like a religious rite, this nightly national ceremony focuses on life and death, by offering the celebrants a succession of flesh films and meat movies. The mood is wild and Dionysian; hidden in their autos, the participants drift into dreamlike, ecstatic trances as forbidden mysteries are revealed and taboos violated on screen.
—Lew Brighton,
"Saturn in Retrograde"

Be bold, be bold, but not too bold,
Lest that your heart's blood should run cold.
—From the story "Mr. Fox," in Joseph Jacobs, English Fairy-Tales *(1898)*

Making filmgoers jump—out of their seats if possible—is, of course, one of the primary ambitions of most horror movie directors (though few are prepared to go to the same lengths as the legendary William Castle, who, for his 1959 schlock classic *The Tingler,* came up with the clever idea of installing electric joy buzzers in the seats). Of all the startling moments in recent American terror films (as S. S. Prawer calls them),[1] perhaps the one that comes closest to fully realizing this worthy goal—i.e., that of getting the audience to respond in roughly the same way as the frog in Galvani's experiment—is the climax of Brian De Palma's *Carrie* (1976), when the dead heroine's arm suddenly erupts from the grave.

To a certain extent, there's no mystery about what makes this scene so jolting. The sequence is the cinematic equivalent of a jack-in-the-box, a mechanism constructed solely for the purpose of giving unsuspecting onlookers a start. De Palma beguiles us with lush, romantic music and a picture-pretty image: Carrie's only friend, flowers in hand, approaches the grave in lyrical, gauzy slow motion. Then, when we're least expecting it, up pops the boogeyman.

Still, it's not only the skillful (even sadistic) way the scene is put together that accounts for its impact. After all, there are many other moments in horror films that function in the same way—in essence, by reassuring the viewer that the worst is over and then, when his defenses are down, sneaking up on him in a fright mask and yelling "Boo!" But most of these scenes, even when they do manage to give viewers a turn (I'm thinking, for example, of the "trick" climax, clearly ripped off from De Palma, of Sean Cunningham's *Friday the 13th*), deliver easy, utterly evanescent shocks. In contrast, the ending of *Carrie*, which takes the form of a particularly vivid and harrowing nightmare, leaves us feeling almost as shaken as the dreamer. It would seem that, quite apart from the scene's effectiveness

at catching us off guard, there is something fundamentally unsettling about the image itself: the cursed and tormented girl,
buried but refusing to rest in peace.

To find out what makes the image so disturbing, we might
begin by asking where it comes from, since it has no parallel in
the Stephen King novel on which the movie is based. King's book
does have its own "shocker" ending, but it is of the slightly
timeworn "here-we-go-again" variety: the ominous "epilogue"
which makes it clear that the horror, far from being over, has
only just begun. (Ira Levin uses the identical device at the close
of *The Boys from Brazil,* and Grade-Z 1950s science fiction
films contain any number of variations, my personal favorite
being the blood-curdling technique of flashing the words "The
End?" on the screen as the final image fades to black.)

One possible source of the ending of *Carrie* is the somewhat similar nightmare that climaxes the film version of James
Dickey's *Deliverance* (Pauline Kael was, I believe, the first to
make this connection). We see a water-level view of the river at
night; slowly, a man's arm—presumably that of the slain hill-
billy—breaks the surface and rises menacingly from the depths.
The film cuts suddenly to a shot of Ed Gentry (the character
played by Jon Voight) awakening in terror, and we understand
that he has been in the grip of bad dreams.

But though there are obvious parallels between this (genuinely chilling) sequence and the conclusion of *Carrie,* there are
important differences, too, in terms of the setting, the gen-
der of the corpse, and—most significantly—the psychological
meaning of the nightmare. In the case of *Deliverance,* the
dream is clearly a function of the protagonist's guilt: Gentry,
a decent and civilized soul, is haunted by the memory of the
man he has brutally, if justifiably, killed. In *Carrie,* the situation is entirely different. For a variety of reasons (for example,
the way Carrie is perceived as accursed because of her terrible
telekinetic powers; the awful death she meets at the hands

of her fanatical mother, who comes to regard the girl as sin-hardened and irreclaimable), the fantasy image De Palma uses to cap his movie suggests a darker, more disquieting complex of meanings.

Interestingly (and unexpectedly), a parallel image, much closer to *Carrie* in every respect than the ending of *Deliverance*, does exist, not in another piece of pop-horror but in the *Nursery and Household Tales* of the Brothers Grimm. The image appears in a fairy tale called "The Willful Child," which is short enough to be quoted in its entirety (indeed, the tale consists of little more than this particular image):

> Once upon a time there was a child who was willful, and would not do what her mother wished. For this reason, God had no pleasure in her, and let her become ill, and no doctor could do her any good, and in a short time she lay on her death-bed. When she had been lowered into her grave, and the earth was spread over her, all at once her arm came out again, and stretched upwards, and when they had put it in again and spread fresh earth over it, it was all to no purpose, for the arm always came out again. Then the mother herself was obliged to go to the grave and strike the arm with a rod, and when she had done that, it was drawn in, and then at last the child had rest beneath the ground. [2]

The parallels between *Carrie* and this grisly little cautionary tale are notable. Though De Palma's movie, following King, possesses a sentimentality wholly missing from the Grimm story (Carrie is portrayed as pathetic, persecuted, and misunderstood), both works center on the figure of a young girl who, having incurred the displeasure of God by disobeying her mother, is punished by death for her iniquity. As for the image of the arm protruding from the ground: the illustration which accompanies this tale in the Pantheon edition of Grimm's—a

"The Willful Child." Illustration by Josef Scharl from Joseph Campbell, The Complete Grimm's Fairy Tales *(1944). Reprinted by permission of Pantheon Books.*

line drawing of a grave with the dead girl's hand jutting out of it—might almost be a storyboard sketch from the climactic sequence of *Carrie.*

What are we to make of this striking correspondence? It seems highly unlikely that "The Willful Child"—in many respects one of the slightest and certainly one of the most obscure tales in the Grimm Brothers' collection—served as either source or inspiration for De Palma. A more plausible explanation, and one which goes a long way toward accounting for *Carrie's* power not only to provide us with a fleeting funhouse thrill but to touch some sort of deep psychic nerve, is that the dream sequence and the *märchen* derive from a common source: from that "symbol-inventing" level of the mind[3] that is the matrix of all folk-dream and myth, the place (to lift a line from Emily Dickinson) "where the Meanings are."[4] That De Palma and the unknown storyteller, diving into that reservoir, should come up with the same compelling image is not surprising, since both artists are engaged in creating essentially the same type of fiction, one intended to elicit an intense combination of wonder and fear.

What we have in the contemporary terror film *Carrie*, then, is a work which, for all its gloss, sophistication, and unabashed commercialism, is a close analogue of a traditional folk tale. Looking at other recent works of pop-horror in light of this fact, we find similar correspondences. *Friday the 13th,* for example (about a group of youngsters who venture into a gloomy forest and encounter a murderous Terrible Mother), is essentially a splatter-movie retelling of "Hansel and Gretel." *The Howling—* a contemporary werewolf movie which, thanks partly to a sly and witty screenplay by John Sayles and partly to some blood-curdling special effects, manages to work as both social satire and seriously scary fright film—has connections to both "The Three Little Pigs" and "Little Red Riding Hood." Indeed, the movie itself draws attention to these links: in one scene we catch glimpses of a TV screen showing Disney's famous "Silly Symphonies" version of "The Three Little Pigs." In a similar way, Stephen King, in his horror novel *Cujo,* lets us know from the start exactly what kind of story we're dealing with. The opening words of the book, printed by themselves on the first page, are "Once upon a time."

King is even more explicit about the connection between fairy tales and his brand of horror in his chatty book of pop criticism, *Danse Macabre.*[5] Analyzing the kinds of collective fears that terror films give expression to, he identifies two main categories of horror: a type that is "sociopolitical in nature," symbolizing the political, economic, and cultural anxieties of a particular time and place (his examples include *Invasion of the Body Snatchers, The Amityville Horror,* and *The Stepford Wives*), and a second, "considerably deeper," more universal variety which he labels "mythic fairy-tale horror." "This second sort of horror film," he writes, "has more in common with the Brothers Grimm than with the op-ed page in a tabloid paper. It is the B-picture as fairy tale," and to illustrate the point he offers a brief quiz in which he recasts the plots of twenty well-known horror films in the form of capsule fairy tales and challenges the reader to identify their titles. (Example: "Once upon a time some bad people tampered with the oxygen lines in one operating room of a major hospital and a lot of people went to sleep for a long, long time—just like Snow White. Only these people never woke up." Answer: *Coma.*)[6]

According to King, movies of the mythic fairy-tale variety achieve their power by confronting us with the forbidden: "This sort of picture doesn't want to score political points but to scare the hell out of us by crossing certain taboo lines."[7] To look once more at *Carrie*, however—what we see there (and this is true for the film as a whole, not just for its final dream-sequence) is an even more intriguing phenomenon: a pop entertainment which does not simply project nightmares and dabble in dangerous fantasy, but which contains precise parallels to particular and widespread primitive taboos, specifically ones dealing with menstruation and the dead.

The sudden emergence of Carrie's awesome abilities coincides precisely with the appearance of her first period. The flow of blood that streams down her thighs as she showers in the girls' locker room (which the camera, representing the viewpoint of the adolescent male, treats as the high-school equivalent of the Sanctuary of Eleusis, the sacred realm of forbidden female mysteries) is accompanied by the earliest manifestation of her telekinetic power. As her taunting schoolmates crowd around the cowering girl, her terror and fury set off a minor explosion in an overhead light fixture. Within a short time, Carrie is toppling a young tormentor from his bike and shattering mirrors with a glance. This association between Carrie's uncanny energies and the onset of her menses reflects a deep-rooted male attitude toward menstruation, an archaic response neatly summed up in Howard Nemerov's poem "Lore":

> Man walks, I learn, in fear of woman,
> Possession of the constant moon;

Because the moon has strength to summon
Her blood to the full and ebb again,
And gives her strength beyond her own.

A girl, then, Graves writes in his book,
Can fade the purple out of cloth
And tarnish mirrors with her look,
And by the power of her thought
Make one branch grow and another rot.

.   .   .   .

So great the power of her moon
That, as the Talmud said,
If she should walk between two men
And no appropriate prayer is read,
The one of them will drop down dead. [8]

Similarly, the attitude toward the dead which underlies the motif of the hand-that-rises-from-the-grave in both the horror film and the fairy tale parallels that primitive dread of corpses (the archaic "supposition" that even "a dearly loved relative at the moment of his death changes into a demon from whom his survivors can expect nothing but hostility")[9] that Freud discusses in his classic psychoanalytic study, *Totem and Taboo.* Reviewing various anthropological theories concerning "the taboo upon the dead," Freud cites the work of Rudolph Kleinpaul, who writes of the belief, common "among the civilized races" of the ancient world, "that the dead, filled with a lust for murder, sought to drag the living in their train."[10] This fantasy, of course, is central to the closing scene of De Palma's film and is portrayed even more explicitly in the newspaper ads for a highly praised 1983 shocker whose very title conveys the essence of those primitive fears and related prohibitions examined by Freud. The movie is called *The Evil Dead,* and the ads for it— clearly inspired by *Carrie*—show a corpse's arm thrust out of

Poster art from The Evil Dead. © *1983 New Line Cinema. Reprinted by permission.*

the earth, its hand clutching the throat of a screaming woman, who is being drawn slowly down into the grave. [11]

Beneath the more superficial aspects of Carrie, then (beyond the things we can say about De Palma's jazzy style and obsessive themes, about the insights the film affords into adolescent sexual anxieties and our society's attitudes toward women), lies a cluster of images that does not reflect the filmmaker's artistic intent, personal unconscious, or cultural conditioning but that emanates from a deeper and far more ancient source, from that immemorial dreaming self that is common to us all; indeed, that is the dark and fertile subsoil out of which our individual identities spring. Such imagery tantalizes us and tempts us toward rational explication. But this is a temptation which should, I believe, be strenuously resisted, since it stems in essence from the deep insecurity which our contemporary waking minds feel in the presence of the mythic.

This kind of discomfort is by no means a universal human trait. As Joseph Campbell points out, the motifs of myth and folk tale are "phrases from an image-language, expressive of metaphysical, psychological, and sociological truth. And in the primitive, oriental, archaic, and medieval societies this vocabulary was pondered and more or less understood. Only in the wake of the Enlightenment has it suddenly lost its meaning and been pronounced insane."[12]

Reviving our ability to understand this language, curing what Australian critic David Tacey calls our "imaginal illiteracy," requires first that we find ways of recognizing the myths embedded in our fictions, and second that we fight against the impulse—indeed, compulsion—to rationalize myth away in terms that offer the conscious mind the comforting illusion that it has gotten to the bottom of mythic meaning. (After all, does it really "explain" the symbol of a magical, singing toad, possessor of the finest carpet, most precious ring, and loveliest maiden in the world to say, as Bruno Bettelheim does in *The Uses of Enchantment*, that "frogs symbolize the id"?)[13]

The second of these goals is, in many ways, the more difficult, since, to achieve it, we must overcome our deeply imagined distrust and denigration of intuition (a form of knowledge typically derided in our culture as "female," the ultimate patriarchal putdown) and our correspondingly exaggerated elevation of intellect as the only legitimate means of uncovering truth. Simultaneously, it requires that we cultivate an ability to (as Campbell says) "ponder" and open ourselves up to the emotional "meaning" of the image: to let the symbol speak for itself.

As for the first prerequisite (seeing the myth to begin with), the most effective method is the one Jungians call "amplification," which consists in essence of drawing out the meaning of a symbol by looking at it in light of analogous myths. The term strikes me as particularly apt, since it suggests an aural metaphor; that is, a correspondence between the method and a mode of nonrational apprehension, of perception and understanding, every bit as valid and precise as logic. The process can be likened to being on a busy street and suddenly finding yourself stirred or unsettled by what you come to recognize as an alien yet strangely familiar melody which you can dimly discern behind the distracting clamor of the city noises. The full meaning of this melody can only be experienced in one way: by getting as close as you possibly can to the source and then listening intently to what the music has to say.

To speak in terms of music, even metaphorically, seems vastly inappropriate when the subject is Tobe Hooper's *The Texas Chain Saw Massacre*, a movie in which the dominant sounds are tortured shrieks, terrified moans, bestial grunts, lunatic laughter, and the incessant, inescapable roar of the titular weapon. The film has become a virtual byword for cinematic sadism gone wild, a prototype of that uniquely contemporary genre of horror picture which is known by its fond admirers as the splatter movie, and which, in the words of writer John Mc-Carty, strives "not to scare . . . audiences, necessarily, nor to drive them to the edge of their seats in suspense, but to *mortify* them with scenes of explicit gore. In splatter movies, mutilation is . . . the message." [14]

Interestingly, however, *The Texas Chain Saw Massacre* contains very little "explicit gore," not only in relation to such cheerfully demented splatter epics as *Bloodthirsty Butchers*, *I Eat Your Skin*, and *2000 Maniacs*, but, indeed, even when compared to the average, contemporary Hollywood action/adventure flick: *48 Hours*, say, or *Rambo: First Blood, Part II.* Though a good deal of dismemberment takes place in Hooper's film, none is ever shown, and there is only one (extremely brief) shot of a chainsaw actually cutting into human flesh, when a fleeing trucker flings a monkey wrench at the head of his pursuer, a squealing, subhuman hulk called Leatherface, who topples to the ground, dropping the blade of his buzzing weapon across his thigh. Considering the kinds of atrocities routinely portrayed in splatter movies (disembowelment, decapitation, castration, amputation, to name just a few of the more run-of-the-mill outrages), it's no wonder that Stephen King says of *Chainsaw*'s director that "Hooper . . . in his own queerly apt way, works with taste and conscience."[15]

But it isn't, of course, Hooper's taste or conscience, any more than the film's (minimal) gore, that has made *The Texas Chain Saw Massacre* a cult movie classic, or that makes sitting through it a kind of *rite de passage*, a test of the horror fan's true mettle and commitment. If the movie strikes a particularly deep and resonant chord, it does so, I submit, because, like *Carrie*, it draws its power not from its immediate, modern-day source but from that timeless place far below the level of consciousness which is the universal wellspring of symbol and myth.

The original ads for *Chain Saw* titillate customers with the venerable freakshow promise that the monstrous display being offered for their entertainment is totally authentic: "What happened is true," the ad reads. "Now see the motion picture that's just as real." And in fact there *is* a real-life basis for the film: the case of the notorious murderer-necrophile Ed Gein, whose grisly crimes also served as the inspiration for Robert Bloch's *Psycho*.

In November 1957, Frank Worden, owner of the local hardware store in the tiny Wisconsin town of Plainfield, returned from a daylong deer-hunting trip to find his mother, Berenice (who had been tending the store in his absence), missing. Various clues led the police to Gein, generally regarded as a harmless, rather affable oddball who picked up extra money doing handyman jobs for his neighbors and otherwise kept pretty much to himself on the 160-acre farm he'd lived on alone since the death of his beloved mother ten years before.

There, in a dingy woodshed attached to the house, the police found Mrs. Worden's headless body, butchered and hung by its heels from a pulley in the ceiling. Inside the house they found even more ghastly remains: A bone-littered floor. A bowl full of noses. A refrigerator stocked with human viscera—hearts, lungs, livers—all neatly wrapped in brown butcher's paper. A saucepan holding a human heart (later identified as Berenice Worden's). A shoebox containing a collection of female genitalia. A pair of lips dangling from the pullstring of a window shade. A chair upholstered in human skin. Soup bowls made from the sawed-off crowns of human skulls. The faces of nine women, carefully dried, stuffed with paper, and mounted, like hunting trophies, on a wall. A skin-vest, complete with breasts, which had been fashioned from the tanned upper half of a middle-aged woman's torso. (Gein later confessed that, on some nights, he would lace the vest around himself and pretend he was his mother.)

Gein's ghoulish crimes, which began with grave robbing and evolved into murder after he'd exhausted the available supply of female corpses in local cemeteries, garnered him nationwide headlines, an eight-page spread in *Life* magazine, and a form of pop immortality, since there is little doubt that, in the fictional guise of Norman Bates, he will continue to haunt the dreams of filmgoers for a long time to come. (Gein himself was promptly shipped off to a state mental institution, where he died in July 1984.) And the true story of his "bizarre and brutal" crimes, as *The Texas Chain Saw Massacre* is described in the ads, promises to play forever on the midnight movie circuit.

In spite of the claims made in the ad copy, however, the fact is that the connections between Hooper's movie and the Gein case are really very tenuous. *Chain Saw* deals with the misadventures of five vacationing teenagers who (as Lew Brighton observes in a vivid, engaging essay on the film) commit the cardinal Texas sin of trespassing on someone else's property, [16] thereby running afoul of an all-male clan of demented former slaughterhouse workers. The patriarch of the group is a virtually mummified old grandpappy who shows few if any vital signs until he's called upon to suck blood from the sliced finger of a captive nymphet. The remaining psychos are three (apparent) brothers: a sniveling, lank-haired creep who wears an animal-skin purse around his neck in which he carries his prized Polaroid snapshots of butchered steers; a slightly more respectable-looking though equally deranged big-brother type, proprietor of a combination gas station/roadside human-barbecue stand; and the overgrown baby of the bunch, the monstrous chainsaw-slinging Leatherface, who wears a mask of dried human skin, communicates in pig grunts, and spends his free time impaling visitors on meat hooks and converting them into assorted prime cuts.

The only ways in which this consummate teenage slice 'n' dice picture—"the *Gone with the Wind* of meat movies," Brighton calls it [17]—resembles the Gein horrors are in its treatment of the victims as so many sides of beef; its attendant cannibal fixation (Gein, in his neighborly way, periodically provided his acquaintances with packages of fresh "venison," though he later testified in court that he had never hunted deer); the human-skin deathmask that gives Leatherface his nickname; and the utterly demented decor found inside in the seemingly innocent white clapboard house that Leatherface and his kinfolk inhabit. Like the rooms in Gein's home (all, that is, except his dead mother's bedroom, which Ed neatly sealed off, preserving it as a shrine to the memory of that God-fearing woman, who taught him to regard all other members of her sex as vessels of sin), the interior of the *Chain Saw* death-house is a chaos of skulls, bones, body parts (in one scene we catch glimpses of an armchair with real human arms), furniture upholstered in human skin, and a wall-to-wall carpet of nameless filth. One of Hooper's real achievements in the movie is creating a visual atmosphere so palpably sickening that the stench of the charnel house seems to waft off the screen.

The power of Hooper's movie, then, clearly has very little to do with its ostensible true-life source. The Gein story casts the same morbid spell as the case histories recorded by Krafft-Ebbing (Ed could easily have stepped out of the pages of *Psychopathia Sexualis*), but to locate the source of *Chain Saw*'s fascination we have to look somewhere else.

To a certain extent, Hooper's film functions as the kind of sociopolitical allegory that Stephen King identifies as one of the two main categories of cinematic horror. Released in 1974 and made by a young man whose only previous feature, an extremely obscure picture called *Eggshells*, focused on the antiwar movement, *Chain Saw* can be viewed as a Vietnam-era vision of America's killer side. *Chain Saw*'s cannibal clan—three brothers and their venerated patriarch (once "the fastest cattle slaughterer in the land")—is a kind of nightmare version of the Cartwright family from "Bonanza": Ben, Little Joe, Adam, and Hoss, those quintessentially decent Americans exposed as a pack of cretinous butchers and their little house on the prairie as nothing more than an abattoir with a porch swing.

Indeed, the 1970s produced two complementary kinds of horror films reflecting the mutually paranoid fantasies of Establishment and countercultural America. The first, exemplified by the Grade-Z gore-fest *I Drink Your Blood* (1971) and culminating in Wes Craven's harrowing *The Hills Have Eyes* (1977), deals with a Manson-like family of cannibal killers that preys on members of the hardhat community and other all-American "straights." *The Texas Chain Saw Massacre* is the prime example of the opposite type, in which a band of innocent youngsters identified with hippie culture through a variety of signs (their van, clothes, hair styles, interest in astrology, etc.) falls victim to a family of working-class crazies from the American heartland.

Chain Saw also exemplifies another intriguing aspect of countercultural fantasy—its evolution (or degeneration) into horror-porn nightmare, a seemingly paradoxical phenomenon which bears out Leslie Fiedler's notion that the function of all truly popular art is "to express the repressed: especially the dark side of our ambivalence toward what any status quo demands we believe, and more often than not, think we do":

> In patriarchal ages, therefore, literature pays tribute to the matriarchal, even as in Christian times it gives the Devil his due. In societies that honor heterosexual bonding and the nuclear family, it allows us to acknowledge men's hatred of women and women's contempt for men, along with the desire of parents to possess utterly or to destroy their children, and the corresponding Oedipal dream of those children. Whatever is officially defined at a given moment as abhorrent to civility and humanity is what such art celebrates, and what is most generally banned is therefore its most nearly universal subject: the impulse to cannibalism, for instance, and incest, the lust to rape and be raped. [18]

In the same way, the orthodoxies of the sixties youth movement—its single-minded insistence that "all you need is love"—ended up generating intense, compensatory fantasies of sadism and ultraviolence, embodied, for example, in the theatrical atrocities of rock star Alice Cooper, who rose to prominence by singing about "Dead Babies" and butchering live chickens on stage; in the nightmare visions of "underground" cartoonists like S. Clay Wilson and Richard Corben; and in the cinematic Grand Guignol of campus favorites like *Night of the Living Dead* and *The Texas Chain Saw Massacre*. As the sleep of reason produces monsters, so, it would seem, the sleep of flower power bred splatter.

Still, while *The Texas Chain Saw Massacre* offers us insight into the collective imagination of young Americans during the Vietnam years, we obviously can't explain the movie's popularity in 1982—when, as Jim Hoberman and Jonathan Rosenbaum report in their book *Midnight Movies, Chain Saw* "became the best-selling home-video cassette" in the country [19]—by pointing to the way the film expressed widespread cultural anxieties a decade earlier. To find a clue to *Chain Saw*'s continuing appeal, we have to look back: beyond the sociopolitical situation that prevailed at the time it was made and that it (inevitably) reflects, beyond the sensational crimes of the late 1950s that supplied some of its superficial details—back, indeed, to the same age-old source that our analysis of the ending of *Carrie* ultimately led us to. For at the core of *The Texas Chain Saw Massacre* and accounting, I believe, for a great deal of its impact is an archetypal motif found in scores of stories throughout the world and powerfully embodied, like the nursery-tale analogue to De Palma's film, in one of the folk narratives recorded by Jacob and Wilhelm Grimm.

That motif is known to folklorists as the Forbidden (or Bloody) Chamber. In a long essay on the subject in the 1885 issue of the *Folk-Lore Journal*, British scholar Edwin Sidney Hartland presents a large number of variants assembled from around the world, introducing them with a quote from a colleague that summarizes the motif in typically prim Victorian terms: "'It is a peculiarity of Fairyland,' says Mr. Clouston in a note to his useful edition of *The Book of Sindbad*, 'that there are certain rooms which the fortunate mortal who has entered the enchanted palace is expressly forbidden to enter, or doors which he must on no account open, or cabinets which he must not unlock, if he would continue in his present state of felicity.'" [20]

Of the different categories of Forbidden Chamber tales identified by Hartland, the best known is the "Bluebeard" type, repre-

The Bloody Chamber. Illustration from Bluebeard: or, The Fatal
Effect of Curiosity and Disobedience *(London, 1808). Reprinted
by permission of the Pierpont Morgan Library, New York.*

sented in the Grimm Brothers' collection by the powerfully unsettling story "Fitcher's Bird." Here a young woman unlocks the
one door that her wizard husband, before leaving on a brief
journey, forbade her to enter in his absence: "But what did she
see when she went in? A great bloody basin stood in the middle
of the room, and therein lay human beings, dead and hewn to
pieces, and hard by was a block of wood, and a gleaming axe lay
upon it." When her husband returns and discovers her disobedience, he wastes no time in taking his revenge: "'Since you
have gone into the room against my will,' said he, 'you shall go
back into it against your own. Your life is ended.' He threw her
down, dragged her along by her hair, cut her head off on the
block, and hewed her in pieces so that the blood ran on the
ground. Then he threw her into the basin with the rest."[21]

This fantasy, of course, is central to *The Texas Chain Saw*

Massacre: indeed, it is the very essence of this movie, in which the victims venture into a place they have been warned is off-limits ("You don't want to go foolin' around other folks' property," advises the kindly gas station owner, who later turns out to be one of the cannibal killers) and are instantly translated from their "present state of felicity" into a state somewhat resembling that of the offerings in the fresh meat section of the local supermarket. Pam, the first of the female victims in the movie, tries to escape after discovering the horrors contained within the house, only to be seized by the monster and, like the luckless young woman in "Fitcher's Bird," dragged back into the death chamber.

There are other similarities between details of Hooper's movie and those of various folk stories that Hartland discusses. In certain tales of the Forbidden Chamber variety, for example, the antagonist is not a single villain but an "ogre [who] is the head of a band of assassins"[22]—a situation very much like the one portrayed in *Chain Saw,* where the chief executioner of the demented clan is the hideous Leatherface. In another variant, the protagonist—in this case a woman (though, as Hartland points out, the victims are frequently males)[23]—is led to disaster by a "hollow groaning" issuing from somewhere in the castle. "The heroine, hearing the groaning and tracing it to the Forbidden Chamber, is overcome by curiosity and opens the door."[24] There is a close analogy to this in Hooper's film, in the killing of the first victim, Kirk, who, hearing strange animal noises coming from a mysterious room, walks over to investigate and is instantly slain by Leatherface, who leaps out and smashes the boy's skull with a sledgehammer. The victim collapses—dead, though still convulsing—across the doorsill: another image paralleled in one of the variants noted by Hartland, in which the victim "opens the door [of the Forbidden Chamber] and falls dead on the threshold."[25]

Cannibalism is implied in many of the tales collected by

Hartland, and in the Grimm Brothers' story "The Robber Bridegroom" (another "Bluebeard" analogue, though one that does not contain the image of the Forbidden Chamber) this theme is treated very explicitly. Here a beautiful maiden is betrothed to a sinister stranger who turns out to be the leader of a gang of cannibals. Spying on the "godless crew" from behind a "great hogshead," the heroine sees them drag home "another young girl. They were drunk, and paid no heed to her screams and lamentations. They gave her wine to drink, three glasses full, one glass of white wine, one glass of red, and a glass of yellow, and with this her heart burst in twain. Thereupon they tore off her delicate raiment, laid her on a table, cut her beautiful body in pieces, and strewed salt thereon."[26] Toward the end of *Chain Saw*, the massacre's only survivor, a pretty blonde teenager named Sally, also witnesses a cannibal feast when she is forced by her captors to sit at the table while they dine on the remains of her friends.

Finally, there is the common motif of the protagonist's ultimate escape, which Hartland refers to as "the flight of the heroine."[27] *Chain Saw*, too, ends with this image, when Sally, battered, bloody, and in hysterics, manages nevertheless to break out of the death-house and elude her berserk, chainsaw-wielding pursuer.

Psychologists of both Freudian and Jungian persuasions have tried their hands at explicating the meaning of the Forbidden Chamber myth. The results have been less than satisfactory, though they do have the virtue of neatly illustrating the limitations of the respective methodologies. Bettelheim, for instance, does his best to rationalize the fundamentally horrific story of "Fitcher's Bird" into yet another safely domesticated, easily understandable, morally edifying fable, a tale designed to inculcate a "higher . . . humanity" by warning: "Women, don't give in to your sexual curiosity; men, don't permit yourself to be carried away by your anger at being sexually betrayed."[28] Un-

The Bloody Chamber in the comics. Panels from "Head Room,"
Haunt of Fear *24 (1954). © 1987 by William Gaines. Reprinted*
by permission.

fortunately, it is hard to fit an image as ghastly as the "corpse
chamber" (to use another of Hartland's vivid phrases) into such
an uplifting reading, so Bettelheim is compelled not simply to
underplay its significance (virtually to the point of ignoring it)
but to misrepresent it as well, referring to it as a "room full of
dead people" when, to be exact, it is a room full of hacked and
dismembered bodies (including those of the heroine's own sis-
ters) and certainly the most nightmarish and haunting detail
in the story, indeed perhaps in the whole of Grimm.

Analytical psychology fares no better than Freudian psychoanalysis. Marie-Louise von Franz, one of the old-guard Zurich luminaries and a specialist in fairy tales, reduces "Bluebeard" to an intrapsychic allegorical drama featuring the usual cast of Jungian personifications, so that the figure of the wife-butcher/cannibal-monster/necrophile turns out to be the "ferocious aspects of the animus in his most diabolical form" in a tale whose (supposed) unconscious intent is "to show how a woman can deal with this inner figure."[29]

Though Hartland himself announces his intention to "arrive at a rational explanation of the origin, evolution, and meaning" of the motif, his article does not really go much beyond collecting examples. Still, he does offer a suggestive clue to the meaning when he observes that "the myth of the Forbidden Chamber is one of a large class which finds its central thought in a taboo."[30] Indeed, like the earlier Grimm story we looked at, the tale of "Fitcher's Bird" seems to embody a very precise and widespread taboo, one having to do, not with menstruation or the dead, but with human sacrifice, and even more specifically with the kind of human sacrifice in which the victim's corpse is ritually cannibalized. Well documented in anthropological literature,[31] this type of taboo is graphically described near the end of Herman Melville's *Typee* in a passage with interesting parallels to the fairy tale motif of the Forbidden Chamber. Exploring the "Taboo Grove" on the day following a "hideous rite" which he has not been permitted to witness, the narrator, Tommo, notices "a curiously carved vessel of wood, of considerable size, with a cover placed over it":

> . . . prompted by a curiosity I could not repress, in passing it I raised one end of the cover; at the same moment the chiefs, perceiving my design, loudly ejaculated, "Taboo! taboo!" But the slight glimpse sufficed; my eyes fell upon the disordered members of a human skeleton, the bones still fresh with moisture, and with particles of flesh clinging to them here and there![32]

In spite of the outcries, then, of right-minded critics like Gene Siskel and Roger Ebert, who denounce splatter films in general as a symptom of a profound cultural neurosis, it is clear that *The Texas Chain Saw Massacre* is no aberration but a cinematic variant of a story far older than the cinema itself— and, indeed, not even one of the grislier variants. (There is nothing in Hooper's movie to compare, for example, to the scene in "Bloudie Jack of Shrewsberrie," one of Richard Harris Barham's popular *Ingoldsby Legends* [1860], in which the heroine discovers a locked cabinet containing the amputated "wedding fingers" and severed "great-toes" of the villain's previous brides.)[33] Since myths can only appear clothed in the cultural trappings of a particular time and place, the superficial details of the story have changed: The deranged aristocrat (or wizard) in his enchanted castle is now a family of rustic, blue-collar crazies living in a farmhouse in cattle country, U.S.A., and the instrument of destruction has evolved from an elegant medieval weapon, a "gleaming axe," into a revved-up, gas-powered McCulloch. But the archetypal essence of the story remains the same.

In a very real sense, the appeal of Hooper's movie—the fascination it exerts—is beyond rational comprehension. But that is just the point. If we are to grasp the meaning of *The Texas Chain Saw Massacre* at all, we have to suppress our rationalizing tendencies and recognize the movie for what it is: a fairy tale, a "form of entertainment" that communicates in the primordial "picture-language of myth."[34] Approaching a work like *Chain Saw* in this way is, for most of us, an extremely difficult task, since it means unlocking a perceptual door which, like the heroes of "Bluebeard," "Fitcher's Bird," and countless other tales of this type, we have been warned against entering—in our case, by a culture which, having lost its sense of the value and meaning of myth, offers us no key.

3 The Giant's Toy

Thumbling in Suburbia

It's conventional these days to see fifties sci-fi and horror films as the product of Cold War anxiety and paranoia—sociopolitical parables in B-movie guise. Peter Biskind's *Seeing Is Believing,* a study of the way the "political tensions of the decade" were reflected in Hollywood genre films, is typical of this tendency. Biskind takes it as axiomatic that "fifties films generally reflected the anticommunism of an anticommunist decade, that sci-fi was a covert meditation on the Bomb, and that aliens, consciously or unconsciously, were equated with Reds."[1] His allegorical reading of the original *Invasion of the Body Snatchers* as a right-wing fantasy epitomizes his approach:

> The pod society is the familiar mechanistic utopia usually (and rightly) taken as a metaphor for Communism. This is a world in which "everyone is the same," a collectivist millennium to which all citizens contribute, as they do here, systematically distributing pods in a parody of political activism. But to the right, this rationalist world in which the head rules the heart, and people act like robots is the dream of the "creeping socialist" center, with its statists and planners, as well as the left. In 1957, for example, *National Review* publisher William Rusher wrote that "the Liberal Establishment . . . shares Communism's materialist principles."

Both *Invasion* and *Them!* imagine attacks from exotic aliens, but the issue at stake in the two films is who's right, the individual or the group, and who commands authority, amateurs or experts, the people or the state. *Invasion* challenges the government's monopoly on wisdom and violence—the reassuring cross-cutting to Washington that characterized *Them!* is simply absent. Individuals must not only act for themselves, they must think for themselves as well. The fact that the hero succeeds in convincing his neighbors he's right is not an expression of the radical right's populist optimism, but also a rehabilitation of common sense, discredited by the center. . . .[2]

Applying a little common sense of his own, Stephen King offers a level-headed rebuke to such reductionism in his critical survey of the horror field, *Danse Macabre*. While King himself argues that certain horror movies function as "disguised comments on the social and political scene,"[3] he maintains that what makes *Invasion* so effective is not its supposed political message (which in any case is so highly ambiguous that the film is also commonly seen as a left-wing attack on McCarthyism) but rather the deep and irreducible appeal of its storyline. Insisting on the paramount importance of story not only to *Invasion* but to all pop writing, King cites the supporting testimony of Jack Finney, author of the original *The Body Snatchers* (the book on which the two movie versions were based), who responds to the various high-flown interpretations of his tale with the good-natured disdain that is characteristic of pop entertainers whose work has been canonized by the critical elite: "I have read explanations of the 'meaning' of this story, which amuse me, because there is no meaning at all; it was just a story meant to entertain, and with no more meaning than that."[4]

There's no reason not to take Finney at his word. After all, assuming they are averse to starvation, paperback writers specializing in horror, sci-fi, or the other pop genres generally favor entertaining narratives over allegorical pokes at centrist ideology. It also seems self-evident to me that any movie as intensely nightmarish as *Invasion of the Body Snatchers* has got to be "about" something besides the political tensions of three decades ago. Certainly it isn't the film's political meaning that makes it so scary to TV audiences today—generally teenage viewers who encounter it for the first time on late-night creature-feature shows and who couldn't care (or know) less about the fifties.

In short, King's assertion that writers like Finney (and himself, for that matter) are in the business of selling stories, not ideas ("plain fiction for plain folk," is one way King has put it in the past),[5] seems not only sensible but inarguable to me. All I would add is that, by and large, these stories turn out to be the very ones that have always provided simple "wonder and entertainment"[6] to the folk. Writing about the Grimm Brothers' story "The Sea-Hare," eminent folklorist Stith Thompson remarks that "the tale is made up of a great many motifs which are . . . folktale commonplaces."[7] The same observation might be made about the majority of pop narratives. While, on one level, *Invasion of the Body Snatchers* is clearly a product of fifties America, its underlying story is compounded of two narrative ingredients known throughout the world and cataloged in Thompson's standard *Motif-Index of Folk-Literature* under the headings "Transformation: Man to Vegetable Form" (Motif D210) and "Plant Causes Magic Forgetfulness" (Motif D1365.1).[8] As their widespread distribution attests, there is something strangely appealing about these story elements, and the effectiveness of *Invasion* can be attributed in large part, I would argue, to its compelling (if unwitting) use of these motifs. In short, like so much contemporary science fiction, *Invasion of the Body Snatchers* is essentially an age-old folktale decked out in space-age garb.

It's also true, however, that the folktales of any society inevitably tell us a great deal about its prevailing conditions and concerns. In *The Uses of Enchantment,* Bruno Bettelheim devotes a chapter to "The Fantasy of the Wicked Stepmother," in which he explains the symbolic meaning of that stock fairy tale character in terms of projection, ambivalence, and related psychoanalytical concepts.[9] But Iona and Peter Opie offer an equally important insight when they point out that "the prevalence of stepmothers [in fairy tales] is accounted for by the shortness of life in past times, by the consequent shortness of marriages, and by the practice of the surviving partner marrying again without unnecessary delay."[10] The point is that the fantasies contained in folk literature always appear in forms that reflect a specific time and place. Thus, the "magic forgetfulness" formerly produced by supernatural plants is blamed, in the era of *Sputnik* and the Cold War, on the insidious influence of evil pods from outer space; and the metamorphosis of a full-grown man into a homunculus, which, in the sixteenth century, would have been imputed to the power of a witch, becomes, in the science fiction of the 1950s, a by-product of radioactive fallout.

Jack Arnold's *The Incredible Shrinking Man* (1957), about a strapping six-footer who is exposed to radioactivity and finds himself, one year later, living in a dollhouse and doing battle with the family cat, vividly illustrates the affinities between what highbrow critics continue to call "pop-cult teen-age junk"[11] and the traditional stories which have delighted human beings for centuries and which these same critics are fond of eulogizing as the naive but noble creations of a pretechnological past. At the start of the movie (based on a book by Richard Matheson, who also wrote the screenplay) we see its hero, Scott Carey, basking on the deck of a pleasure-boat alongside his quintessentially fifties (i.e., blonde, busty) wife, Louise. Seconds after "Lou" goes below to fetch a couple of beers, the boat passes through a mysterious cloud, which leaves a residue of shimmering particles across Scott's chest.

The film then cuts six months ahead. We are in the Carey's cozy, suburban living room, located in that generic Hollywood setting (tree-lined streets, split-level houses, jolly milkman) familiar from countless fifties movies and TV sitcoms. Scott, dressing for work, is scolding his wife for having picked up the wrong clothes from the laundry; his shirt is several sizes too large. Crazy as it seems, he slowly becomes convinced that he is not only losing weight but losing height as well. Ultimately, his condition is confirmed by the specialists, who diagnose it as a "negative nitrogen balance," a rare disorder that happens to people who pass through radioactive clouds after being sprayed with insecticide (Scott, we learn, had received an accidental dousing shortly before leaving on his boating trip). As Stephen King observes in his discussion of Matheson's novel, this unlikely explanation is simply magic masquerading as science, "a mid-twentieth-century version of pentagrams, mystic passes, and evil spells."[12]

Before long, Scott is down to three feet and reduced to wearing kiddie clothes. Sitting on a living room chair in dungarees and polo shirt, his sneakered feet barely reaching the edge of the cushion, he looks like a preschooler. Unable to earn a living, he reluctantly agrees to sell his story to the tabloids. His doctors discover a serum that arrests the course of his disease, and he enjoys an interlude of happiness when he meets and falls in love with a pretty sideshow midget named Clarice. Soon, however, he is shrinking again.

The next scene is a shocker. We see Scott, apparently back to normal size, standing in his living room. Suddenly we become aware that the furnishings are scale-model replicas: he is living in a doll house. Attacked by the family cat, he falls into the basement. The final segment is the most exciting and memorable part of the film. Scott, only inches high, becomes a kind of mini–Robinson Crusoe, struggling to survive in his basement wasteland: stealing food out of mousetraps, scaling mountainous tables to scavenge for crumbs, and battling a monster-sized spider in the film's climactic scene. The quasi-mystical (but strangely moving) ending has Scott dissolving into a nothingness that turns out to be the All, the place, as he puts it, where the infinitesimal and the infinite merge. (In the slightly different but equally upbeat ending of the novel, Scott is reborn into a luminous microscopic wonderland.)

The first thing to be said about *The Incredible Shrinking Man* is that it is one of the most engrossing adventure tales ever put on screen. Like the best fantasy stories, it reawakens our sense of wonder. Indeed, by showing the mundane world (a basement full of household junk) transformed into a realm of marvels, the movie is a kind of metaphor for the fantasy-making process itself, for that basic imaginative act which allows us to turn "banality to magic in a trice" and which underlies every form of human play, from the child's game of "make-believe" to the most elaborate religious festivals. [13]

More specifically, *The Incredible Shrinking Man* is a fantasy with an ancient hold on the imagination of humankind. At one point in the film, when Scott has disappeared into the basement and is presumed dead by the world, his obituary is delivered on TV, and when the commentator describes the tiny hero as someone "whose fantastic story was known to virtually every man, woman, and child in the civilized world," he is speaking more truly than he (or the screenwriter) knows. For *The Incredible Shrinking Man* is, in fact, a modern-day version or reinvention of what is possibly the most enduring of all wonder-tales, "Tom Thumb"—the "prototype fairy tale," in the words of Iona and Peter Opie. [14]

The earliest recorded version of this classic tale appears in a crudely printed pamphlet, *The History of Tom Thumbe, the Little, for His small stature surnamed, King Arthur's Dwarf: Whose Life and adventures containe many strange and wonderful accidents, published for the delight of merry Timespenders* (1621). This title is itself suggestive of the affinities not only between Tom Thumb and Matheson's miniature hero (whose life also consists of a string of strange accidents) but, more generally, between the traditional folk story and contemporary popular narrative. Both forms of fiction, after all, are contrived "for the delight of merry Time-spenders," which is to say that they are "mere" pastimes. Indeed, it is this very quality which, in a culture that equates time with money, makes such unpretentious entertainments seem so trivial to the more serious-minded members of the community, who have little use for any imaginative work that doesn't offer a tangible return on their investment; that is, that doesn't pretend to uplift or improve them in some way. Even so ardent a champion of the wondertale as Bruno Bettelheim takes a purely (indeed, quite narrowly) pragmatic approach to the material, basing his defense of "enchantment" strictly on its therapeutic "uses."

It is important to remember, however, that, as the eminent myth scholar Mircea Eliade points out, one important function of myth is precisely to "waste"—destroy, abolish—time, to transport us to a deathless, eternal world where history is suspended. [15] And that same "magico-religious" function, Eliade argues, is performed in modern-day society by our entertainments, our diversions: by those things we do to "kill time":

The defence against Time which is revealed to us in every kind of mythological attitude, but which is, in fact, inseparable from the human condition, reappears variously disguised in the modern world, but above all in its *distractions*, its amusements. It is here that one sees what radical difference there is between modern cultures and other civilizations. In all traditional societies, every responsible action reproduced its mythical, transhuman model, and consequently took place in sacred time. Labour, handicrafts, war and love were all sacraments. The re-living of that which God and Heroes had lived *in illo tempore* imparted a sacramental aspect to human existence. . . . By thus opening out into the Great Time, this sacramental existence, poor as it might often be, was nevertheless rich in significance; at all events it was not under the tyranny of Time.

The true "fall into Time" begins with the secularisation of work. It is only in modern societies that man feels himself to be the prisoner of his daily work, in which he can never escape from Time. And since he can no longer "kill" time during his working hours—that is, while he is expressing his real social identity—he strives to get away from Time in his hours of leisure: hence the bewildering number of distractions invented by modern civilization. [16]

Elsewhere, Eliade specifically mentions both movies and "literature for mass popular consumption" [17] as examples of those seemingly empty pastimes which, in fact, are the debased, "desacralized," but nevertheless genuine equivalents of traditional mythic narrative. Eliade's point, in short, is that those activities commonly scorned as "mindless escapism" or a "worthless waste of time" are, in fact, a very basic human necessity, a product of our profound desire to break free of the "implacable becoming that leads toward death" and escape to a place where "Time stands still." [18]

In fairy tales this magical land is always located in the distant past and described in a simple, formulaic phrase which varies only slightly from story to story: "Once upon a time," "A long time ago," "In a certain kingdom once," "In olden times," etc. Whatever the wording, the world thus evoked is always the same: that "primordial, paradisaical" [19] realm which, however faraway and fabulous it may seem, is deeply and immediately familiar to us, since it corresponds to the ahistorical consciousness we inhabit in earliest childhood, when time is experienced not (in Robert Penn Warren's memorable image) as "a movement, a flowing, a wind" but rather as "a kind of climate in which things are." [20] The longing for this lost paradise is, perhaps, more central to *The History of Tom Thumbe* than to other fairy tales. Indeed, the story begins on an unusually nostalgic note, wistfully evoking "the old time, when King Arthur ruled this land [and] the World was in a better frame than it is now."[21] More significantly (and in contrast to such classic *märchen* as "The Frog-Prince," "Sleeping Beauty," and "Cinderella," which, according to Bettelheim and like-minded critics, portray the process of maturation), *The History of Tom Thumbe* is explicitly a fantasy about perpetuating the condition of infancy—about staying small—forever. Its hero is a perennial preemie, a child who "comes abortive from [his mother's] wombe"[22] after a three-month gestation and who (though possessed of superior wit and agility) never grows any larger than a miscarried fetus:[23] "The child thus borne . . . had at the first minute it took life, the full and largest bignes that ever it grew to. . . . as he was at the first houre of his birth, so continued he to the last minute of his life" (p. 34).

The story itself is similarly underdeveloped, a rudimentary series of highly (almost obsessively) repetitious "adventures" in which the embryonic hero is reabsorbed into and then rudely expelled from one symbolic womb after another. Following Tom's magical birth (he is brought into being by the "inchanter" Merlin, who grants Tom's plowman father his wish for a son, "though it were no bigger than my thumbe"), the tiny hero is, in rapid succession, imprisoned in a pin box, baked into a black pudding, swallowed (and subsequently excreted) by a cow, trapped in a mousehole, ingested by a giant, and gulped down by a large fish. In "Thumbling," the better-known version of the tale contained in the Grimm Brothers' collection, the title character undergoes a similar set of experiences. "Where have you been, then?" cries Thumbling's father when his child reappears after a prolonged absence. "Ah, father," the manikin replies, "I have been in a mouse's hole, in a cow's belly, and then in a wolf's paunch; now I will stay with you."[24] According to Iona and Peter Opie, "Analysts of the folktale like to point out that Tom's history is one of the swallow cycle; and that it is thus related to the story of Little Red Riding Hood who was devoured by a wolf, a kinship that others may find rather distant. It would seem more apt to describe Tom's history as a swallow cycle in itself."[25]

To be sure, both versions of the story include other types of adventures, in which the Thumbling hero exercises his trickster abilities on various oversized adversaries. *The History of Tom Thumbe* also contains a lengthy interlude in which Tom becomes a gallant at King Arthur's court and a companion of the royal ladies, who like to use him as a plaything:

> . . . the Ladies and Gentlewomen could seldom bee without him; for his company was so pleasing, that many times they gave him leave to sleepe upon their knees, and now and then in their pockets, with many such private places, and withall to sit upon their pinpillows, and play with their pins, and to runne at tilt against their bosomes with a bulrush; for bigger weapon was hee not able to manage. (p. 41)

For the most part, however, Tom's remarkable birth serves as the prototype for his subsequent adventures, which simply repeat, in various symbolic guises, the moment of his miraculous delivery. If characters like Snow White and Cinderella are models of emotional growth and transformation, Tom Thumb, by contrast, undergoes no postnatal development whatsoever. He is stuck in a state of permanent parturition.

As folklore scholars point out, the English *History of Tom Thumbe* is only one of scores of such tales whose antiquity and worldwide distribution attest to the timeless, universal appeal of fantasies about "impossibly small men."[26] In Continental Europe, write the Opies, Tom's counterparts include

> *Le petit Poucet* in France; *Daumesdick, Däumling,* and *Daumerling,* also swallowed by a cow, in Germany; and *Svend Tomling* in Denmark, "a man no bigger than a

thumb, who would be married to a woman three ells and three quarters long." . . . Further afield, the English imp may be compared with *Vamuna* in India, and *Issun Boshi* ("Little One Inch") in Japan, who danced about in an ogre's stomach, jabbing at it with his needle-sword. [27]

There is no way of knowing, of course, whether Richard Matheson had the Thumbling myth in mind when he dreamed up the adventures of Scott Carey. [28] The only fairy tale allusion to be found in *The Incredible Shrinking Man* appears in the original novel, when Scott first encounters the sideshow midget Clarice, whose stage name is "Mrs. Tom Thumb,"[29] a pseudonym which, in any case, refers less to the folklore figure than to P. T. Barnum's pint-size protégé, General Tom Thumb, "the most famous Midget in the modern world."[30] Whatever Matheson's intention, however, his novel—and the movie made from it—clearly represents a striking sci-fi analogue of the traditional wondertale, an updated, distinctly American variant of the archetypal story of Thumbling (Type 700 in the Aarne-Thompson index).

Like the manikin heroes of folklore, Scott Carey must rely on his wits and whatever weapons he can contrive to survive the homespun perils that he is exposed to, the majority of which involve the characteristic threat of being swallowed or sucked down into darkness. Scott, for example, is pursued by a hungry housecat, drawn toward the vortex of a basement drain, and, armed with a pin-sword (like the Japanese "Little One Inch" and the Grimm Brothers' Thumbling, who ventures forth into the world with a blade made from a darning needle), driven to do battle with a devouring insect. In the novel, moreover, Scott becomes trapped in his basement when he is attacked outside his house by a rapacious, dive-bombing bird and makes a desperate leap for safety through a broken cellar window (p. 180). Soon afterward, he encounters a "colossus" (in reality, a normal-size handyman come to repair the water heater) who is as awesome to the inches-high hero as any man-eating storybook giant:

> He had just measured himself at the ruler and was walking back to the water heater when . . . a giant came clumping down the cellar steps. . . . He stood horror-rooted to the spot, staring up at the mammoth figure bearing down on him, its plunging shoes raised higher than his head, then slamming down and shaking the floor beneath him. . . .
>
> Scott ran, splashing, around its right shoe, the top of his head level with the lip of the sole. Standing beside the cement block, he peered up at the colossus.
>
> Far up—so far he had to squint to see—was its face: nose like a precipitous slope that he could ski on; nostrils and ears like caves into which he could climb; hair a forest he could lose himself in; mouth a vast, shut cavern; teeth (the giant grimaced suddenly) he could slide an arm between; eye pupils the height of him, black irises wide enough to crawl through, lashes like dark, curling sabers. (pp. 63–64)

The parallel here between *The Incredible Shrinking Man* and *The History of Tom Thumbe*, in which Tom, after being set upon by a raven, plunges down a chimney and finds himself in the clutches of a "fearefull . . . Gyant" (p. 40), is particularly striking.

In other ways, too, Matheson's work conforms closely to the folkloric pattern. As in various Thumbling stories, both the book and film versions of *The Incredible Shrinking Man* derive a great deal of their enchantment from the details of the mini-hero's daily routines—how he dresses, what he eats, where he sleeps, and so on. Like *The History of Tom Thumbe*, for example, which pays considerable attention to the protagonist's "apparrell" (including his oak leaf hat, shirt sewn from a spider's web, and shoes made out of mouse's hide),[31] Matheson's story describes Scott Carey's ongoing efforts to fashion clothing suitable for his diminutive, and rapidly dwindling, frame (by the end of the novel, even his handkerchief-robe and sandals woven from bits of string have become too large for him). And just as Tom Thumb is shown trapped in a pin-box, dining on the "third part" of a hazel-nut "curnell" and reposing on a pincushion, so Scott Carey finds himself taking refuge in a sewing box, gorging himself on cracker crumbs and sleeping on a sponge. By dwelling on such homely details, *The Incredible Shrinking Man*, like its fairy tale prototype, not only creates a vivid sense of the hero's fantastical tininess but, more significantly, transforms the most ordinary household articles into objects of wonder, endowing the mundane and domestic with an innocent magic and compelling us to see the world through the marveling eyes of a child.

It goes without saying, of course, that, unlike certain other examples of the Thumbling story, *The Incredible Shrinking Man* possesses no cultural prestige whatsoever. The original 1621 *History of Tom Thumbe*, for instance, is part of the J. P. Morgan collection, and interested readers can find it reprinted in Iona and Peter Opie's beautifully produced volume *The Classic Fairy Tales*, published by Oxford University Press. By contrast, copies of *The Incredible Shrinking Man* are generally found only in the collections of aficionados of Grade-B science fiction movies. Anyone else interested in seeing the film has to keep an eye peeled for its occasional appearance on midnight TV monster shows, where it is generally shown as part of a double bill with pictures like *The Brain Eaters* and *It! The Terror from beyond Space*.

Nevertheless, of all the existing variants of the Thumbling legend, the movie version of *The Incredible Shrinking Man* is, to my mind, the most genuinely marvelous (in the strict sense of the term), partly because, being a movie, it can exploit a type of magic unavailable to other more traditional modes of storytelling; that is, the magic of motion picture special effects. In a very real sense, special effects are a product of the same innate human craving—the same fundamental hunger for miracle and enchantment—that is the source of the fairy tale itself. After all, although George Méliès, the French magician-turned-filmmaker and the so-called father of special effects, is sometimes referred to as the "Jules Verne of the cinema,"[32] his delightfully imaginative trick films (including *Fairyland, The Blue Bird, Cinderella,* and *Red Riding Hood*) are actually in a direct line of descent from the nursery tales of Perrault. Méliès, to my knowledge, never based a movie on "Le Petit Poucet," Perrault's version of the Thumbling legend, known in English as "Hop o' My Thumb," but a number of his filmed "enchantments" did, in fact, exploit a primitive form of split-screen cinematography to portray Thumbling-sized figures. (The best known is probably his 1902 short, *The Dancing Midget,* in which a pocket-size ballerina performs a *pas seul* on the outstretched palm of a spectator.) Throughout motion picture history, this illusion has been central to the fantasy film (*le cinéfantastique,* as the French call it), appearing in a wide range of movies, from cult favorites like *Attack of the Puppet People* (1957) and *The Seventh Voyage of Sinbad* (1958) to such genre classics as *The Bride of Frankenstein* (1935) and *Dr. Cyclops* (1940). No movie, however, contains more compelling miniaturization effects than *The Incredible Shrinking Man,* partly because the film (though shot in black-and-white on an obviously low budget) is a technical *tour de force,* but, even more importantly, because its visual wizardry is used in the service of a story with such deep and persistent appeal. In short, *The Incredible Shrinking Man* represents, if not the culmination of, then certainly a high point in the ongoing effort of filmmakers (beginning with Méliès) to transform technology into magic by using the motion picture camera to make the imaginary wonders of the fairy tale materialize before the very eyes of the viewer.

What makes *The Incredible Shrinking Man* so compelling, however, is not simply its ingenious use of twentieth-century technology to bring the ancient tale of Thumbling to life. After all, in 1958, just one year after the movie's release, a second cinematic version of the fairy tale appeared: *tom thumb*, a lavishly produced (not to say enormously overblown) kiddie picture conceived and directed by fantasy filmmaker George Pal. Although the visual tricks in Pal's extravaganza are more sophisticated than those in Arnold's film (indeed, *tom thumb* won the 1958 Oscar for special effects), the movie is a charmless and plodding affair which takes the Grimm Brothers' story and, in essence, embalms it. Part of the problem with Hollywood "family films" like *tom thumb* is that they conceive of fairy tales as the fictional equivalent of Cabbage Patch dolls—cute and sugary creations designed to warm the hearts of "children of all ages." The fact is, however, that folk stories are not quaint little artifacts but vital products of the human imagination which serve to articulate (and thereby, to some degree, moderate) the communal anxieties of the day by assimilating them into deeply familiar narrative patterns. Thus, as Robert Danton writes in his marvelous study *The Great Cat Massacre*, fairy tales—for all their archetypal underpinning and timeless appeal—are actually "historical documents" produced by born raconteurs who have the natural ability to adapt "an inherited theme" to "their own milieux," so that "the specificity of the time and place shows through the universality of the topos."[33] For this reason, "hack" entertainers like Richard Matheson and Jack Arnold, who exploit the social obsessions of the moment by embodying them in the sure-fire stories that have enthralled audiences for centuries, seem closer to true folk tradition than such self-appointed custodians of the Grimm Brothers' legacy as Walt Disney, George Pal, and, most recently, Shelley Duvall (producer of cable TV's popular "Faerie Tale Theatre").

Critics who concern themselves with Hollywood B-movies tend to lump *The Incredible Shrinking Man* together with other 1950s sci-fi films which reflect that era's acute A-bomb worries: "big bug" pictures like *Them!* (1954) and *The Deadly*

Mantis (1957) or movies like *The Beast from 20,000 Fathoms* (1953), in which prehistoric behemoths, preserved for several million years inside the polar ice, are resuscitated during a nuclear test. Far from being a central concern of *The Incredible Shrinking Man*, however, radioactive poisoning is used by Matheson as nothing more than a flimsy plot device which serves to set Scott's transformation in motion and then disappears more or less entirely as an issue in the film. There *is* a deep anxiety which finds powerful expression in *The Incredible Shrinking Man*, but, although it is no less characteristic of fifties America than the fear of nuclear fallout or creeping communism, it derives from a very different source than Cold War paranoia. It is possible to begin shedding light on this underlying concern by noting two significant ways in which *The Incredible Shrinking Man*—for all its close resemblance to the traditional tellings of "Tom Thumb"—differs from earlier versions of the story, ways which mark Matheson's work as a specifically American, mid-twentieth-century variant of the archetypal tale.

First, although the adventures of the original Tom Thumb are highly repetitious in kind, they occur over a far-flung area, carrying the tiny hero from schoolhouse and cottage to a giant's castle and King Arthur's court (indeed, the sequel to the first Tom Thumb story in the Grimm Brothers' collection is entitled "Thumbling's Travels"). [34] By contrast, Scott Carey's adventures take place almost entirely within the confines of his small suburban home, where, for the better part of the story, he feels (and is) hopelessly entrapped. Second, the fairy tale Tom Thumb is a completely static character, a manikin who never grows "older, nor younger; bigger, nor smaller; stronger, nor weaker" than he is at the moment of birth. [35] The central fact of Scott Carey's existence, on the other hand, is that he starts out as a full-grown man and inexorably dwindles to the size of an embryo, moving back through the various stages of development—from adolescent to toddler to infant—along the way. In short, if *The History of Tom Thumbe* is a dream of eternal childhood, *The Incredible Shrinking Man* is a nightmare of regression—a regression, moreover, that takes place in the context of a specific domestic situation.

That the uneasiness which pervades Matheson's work is connected to marriage has been noted by a number of critics. Speaking of the ways in which certain horror movies articulate "the terrors . . . of our everyday existence," for example, S. S. Prawer observes that "many a man will have recognized his own marriage-problems, in fantastically heightened form, in *The Incredible Shrinking Man.*"[36] Stephen King is a good deal more explicit about the nature of those problems, arguing in *Danse Macabre* that Scott Carey's predicament is, in effect, a metaphor for sexual dysfunction:

> Shrinking itself is an oddly arresting concept . . . Tons of symbolism come immediately to mind, most of it revolving around the potency/impotency thing. . . .
>
> Scott's most painful problems are with Lou, his wife. They are both personal and sexual, and I think that most men, even today, tend to identify the magic most strongly with sexual potency. A woman may not want to but she can; a man may want to and find he cannot. Bad news. And when Scott is 4′ 11″ tall, he comes home from the medical center where he has been undergoing tests and walks straight into a situation where the loss of sexual magic becomes painfully evident. [37]

Though there's some validity to King's point, it's hard not to feel that his reading says more about the obsessions of our own post–Masters and Johnson era than about the preoccupying concerns of post–World War II America, the time in which *The Incredible Shrinking Man* is set. To be sure, Matheson's hero suffers from an acute sense of masculine insecurity. But this feeling, I believe, has less to do with the sort of sexual perfor-

Fantasies of being emasculated by marriage are common in 1950s popular art. In the comic book story "Second Childhood," an elderly scientist, wed to a younger woman, regresses to infancy after injecting himself with a rejuvenating serum. From Weird Fantasy 4 *(1950). © 1987 by William Gaines. Reprinted by permission.*

Scott Carey is not the first shrinking man in 1950s sci fi. In a 1951 issue of the E.C. Comic Weird Fantasy, *Dr. Hugo Masterson is exposed to a radioactive formula designed to reduce cancerous tissue and ends up small enough to be swallowed, in a single gulp, by his wife. © 1987 by William Gaines. Reprinted by permission.*

mance anxiety King perceives than with a fifties phenomenon discussed by various cultural critics; namely, with a fantasy of emasculation which—for reasons having to do with that era's reigning "cult of domesticity"[38]—flourished in the postwar male population.

While the young men who returned from the war and migrated en masse to the suburbs were only too happy to make "mothers of their wives,"[39] their new family-centered existence

seems to have brought with it—along with the desired domestic comforts—deep-seated feelings of diminished or enfeebled
masculinity. These feelings found expression in a particular set
of fantasies of being infantilized, subjugated, and unmanned:
transformed from a potent adult into a household slave or
woman's plaything. [40] Even a cursory glance at the male-
produced pop art of the period indicates just how common
these fantasies were. They appear almost everywhere, from
movies to comic books to popular magazines. *Man's Action,*
Man's Life, and similar pre-*Playboy* publications, for example,
are full of features with titles like "Bashful Brides Have Ruined
the American Male" and "Your Wife Can Destroy Your Sex Confidence." [41] In the 1950s, America's mightiest hero, Superman,
metamorphosed from a "man of steel" into a kind of costumed
super-schnook. Comic book covers of the period show him
using his super-breath to blow out the candles on a birthday
cake, igniting the charcoal for a backyard barbeque with his
heat-vision, and—in one notorious instance—hopping around
in agony after having one of Lois Lane's biscuits dropped on his
big toe. "Like the returning GI's, Superman was absorbed into
the daily routines of civilian life," writes Jim Steranko in his
entertaining *History of Comics.* "The Man of Tomorrow had become the fall guy of today." [42] An even more revealing document
in terms of postwar male self-perception is the popular newspaper strip *Blondie,* whose housebroken hero, according to
Marshall McLuhan, is a true representative man, embodying all
the domestic and economic anxieties of the fifties middle-class
breadwinner:

> Dagwood expresses the frustration of the suburban com-
> muters of our time. . . . His detestation of his job is plain
> in the postponement of the morning departure till there
> comes the crescendo of despair and the turbulent take-off.
> Rising and departure are traumatic experiences for him,

involving self-violence. His swashbuckling, midnight forays to the icebox, whence he returns covered with mayonnaise and the gore of ketchup, is a wordless charade of self-pity and Mitty-Mouse rebellion. Promiscuous gormandizing as a basic dramatic symbol of the abused and the insecure has long been understood.

The number of suburban-marriage strips and radio programs is increasing. Each has the same theme—model mother saddled with a sad sack and a dope. We are confronted on a large scale with what Wyndham Lewis has described as mothering-wedlock. [43]

Fantasies of being emasculated by marriage were particularly rife in Hollywood films of the 1950s, as Peter Biskind makes clear in *Seeing Is Believing.* Citing scores of movies (*Pride of the Marines, Rebel without a Cause, The Snake Pit, A Star Is Born, Red River, Giant,* and dozens more), Biskind traces the transformation of the old-fashioned, "hard as nails" American hero into a browbeaten "momma's boy," inhabiting a culture dominated by "monstrous mother" figures and condemned to a life of perpetual servitude in an imprisoning "suburban dollhouse."[44] The male insecurities Biskind uncovers in mainstream fifties movies are even more apparent in the world of cinematic schlock—specifically, in the spate of poverty row exploitation pictures (many of which have since become cult favorites) involving female giants (*Attack of the 50-Foot Woman,* for example, and *The Thirty Foot Bride of Candy Rock*) or societies populated entirely by Amazons (*Fire Maidens from Outer Space, Cat Women of the Moon, She Demons, Devil Girl from Mars, Love Slaves of the Amazon, Mesa of Lost Women,* etc.).[45] Although Biskind discusses a number of science fiction/horror films in his book (*Them!, The Thing, Invasion of the Body Snatchers, I Was a Teenage Werewolf,* and several others), he says nothing about *The Incredible Shrinking Man*—

*The voyage to a planet populated entirely by women is a wide-
spread motif in 1950s science fiction. Panel art from ". . . For
Posterity,"* Weird Science Fantasy 24 *(1954). © 1987 by William
Gaines. Reprinted by permission.*

a curious omission, since Arnold's movie is arguably the most
striking expression of masculine insecurity to come out of
Hollywood in the fifties, a film which achieves its most unsettling effects by taking common metaphors for male subjugation
(including the metaphors used by Biskind himself) and making
them terrifyingly real.

Some men grow too big for their britches, but when we first
see Scott in his bedroom, dressing for work, it's clear that his
grownup clothes—and the adult responsibilities they signify—
are rapidly becoming too big for him. Like millions of his male
contemporaries, Scott is an ex-GI, a fact revealed early on in the
movie when, alarmed at his inexplicable loss of stature, he vis-
its a doctor and explains that he has not had his height checked
since his draft exam, when he measured over six feet.[46] The
suggestion here is unmistakable: The last time Scott stood tall
was in the military, in the days before his marriage. Scott's fa-
tigues obviously fit him just fine; it's his civilian uniform—the
conservative suit of the solid suburban wage-earner—that he
has begun to have trouble filling.

At first, Scott's wife, Lou, can't believe that he's shrinking, though she grows increasingly concerned as he continues to shed weight. Ironically, her solution to his problem is to treat him like a child. When Scott tells her near the start of the film that he's lost yet another four pounds, she answers in the typically infantilizing terms of fifties "mothering-wedlock": "That's it, my boy. You're going to start taking vitamins. I'll get you so fat on ice cream and cake you'll think you're living in a child's paradise." Given this response (and all that it implies about the nature of Scott's marriage), it's no surprise that his regression continues unchecked. Ultimately, however, Lou's maternal attentions aren't the cause of Scott's problem. What really unmans him is his deflating sense of being unable to fulfill his wife's needs: not her sexual needs (about which virtually nothing is said in either the novel or film), but her material and economic ones, which, to her beleaguered husband, are clearly overwhelming.

Scott's earning power is a major issue in *The Incredible Shrinking Man*, and the film wastes no time in establishing his shortcomings as a provider. When we first see Scott, lolling on the deck of a cabin-cruiser, he is trying to cajole Lou into fetching him a drink. "I provided the boat," he tells her, "so you provide the beer." "Oh, Scott," Lou pointedly answers. "Your brother provided the boat." And indeed, Scott's businessman brother, Charlie (called Marty in the novel), seems to exist for no other reason than to highlight the hero's inadequacy. Scott, it turns out, not only works for Charlie but, more humiliatingly, is obliged to live on his big brother's handouts after shrivelling to child size. Eventually, however, Charlie is forced to remove his sibling from the payroll. The scene in which he informs Scott of this necessity makes the contrast between the two men painfully clear. We see Charlie—a stern, imposing figure decked out in a no-nonsense business suit—looming over the puny hero, who has been reduced to wearing playground clothing and sits hunched in an armchair like a chastised schoolboy who has just had his allowance cut for misbehavior. The scene is a powerful visual metaphor of Scott's economic inferiority, of his sense of financial impotence. In the world of getting and spending, of position, wealth, and power, Scott just doesn't measure up.

Scott's financial anxieties are stressed even more in the book. Throughout the novel, money weighs heavily on his mind. Matheson's hero, we are told early on, has moved from Los Angeles to Long Island with high hopes for getting ahead:

> He was thinking about his application for life insurance. It had been part of his plan in coming East. First working for his brother, then applying for a GI loan with the idea of becoming a partner in Marty's business. Acquiring life and medical insurance, a bank account, a decent car, clothes, eventually a house. Building a structure of security around himself and his family. (pp. 9–10)

Scott's strange affliction, however, inevitably sabotages this scheme. Near the start of the novel, when his condition has been confirmed and his doctor recommends further testing, Scott contemplates his situation with a profound sense of hopelessness:

> "The cost, Lou, the *cost.* It'll take at least a month's hospitalization; Branson said so. A month away from work. Marty's already upset as it is. How can I expect him to go on paying my salary when I don't even—" . . .
> He lowered his head, teeth clenched behind drawn lips. Every bill was a chain that weighed him down. He could almost feel the heavy links forged around his limbs. (p. 9)

Indeed, there is a close, if inverse, relationship between the hero's physical state and economic status: As Scott gets smaller, his money worries increase at a commensurate rate. By the time he is down to thirty-five inches, his situation has grown nearly intolerable: "Days passed, one torture on another. Clothes were taken in for him, furniture got bigger, . . . Lou got bigger. Financial worries got bigger" (p. 81). One doesn't have to be slightly shorter than a yardstick, however, to empathize with Scott. Indeed, what Matheson is describing here—the sense of being overwhelmed by the domestic and monetary burdens of middle-class life—is a chronic complaint of the mid-century American male. One is put in mind of James Thurber's famous cartoon "Home," depicting a fearful little fellow quailing at the prospect of entering his house, which has taken on the lineaments of his enormous, glowering wife. [47] Matheson's conceit is to turn this fantasy into a living nightmare. To a shrinking man, a "mountain of bills" is no mere metaphor but a real— and unscalable—Everest. Scott's ailment, in short, has far less to do with radioactive fallout than with the socioeconomic pressures experienced by the young suburban husbands of his day. [48]

The connection between Matheson's story and Thurber's cartoon is apt for another reason. Although Scott's inadequacy as a wage-earner is underscored by his sibling's success, it is not Charlie/Marty who is at the root of his problems. Rather, it is Lou, who is portrayed in the novel as a stereotypically demanding female, applying pressure on her hapless spouse to provide her with the middle-class comforts she regards as her due. At first, Lou seems genuinely solicitous of Scott and bravely prepared to accept the financial sacrifices that his illness will entail. "Honey, your health comes first," she protests when Scott announces his decision to refuse further medical treatment because of its cost (p. 9). But as the bills mount up and Scott's ability to meet them diminishes, Lou's feelings change dramatically—her sympathy turns into scorn, her concern into bitterness and resentment. Before very long, she begins pressing Scott to exploit his misfortune by selling his story to the tabloids. Scott is incensed: "What would you like me to do—turn myself into a public freak to give you your security?" (p. 14). Lou seems chastened, but by the time Scott has dwindled to the height of an infant, her contempt is undisguised:

> . . . he remembered the day when he had been twenty-eight inches tall, the height of a one-year-old child—a china doll that shaved real whiskers and bathed in a dishpan and used a baby's potty chair and wore made-over baby clothes.
>
> He had stood in the kitchen yelling at Lou because he'd suggested that she put him in a sideshow to make some money and she hadn't insisted that he shouldn't say such things; she'd only shrugged.
>
> He'd yelled and ranted, his little face red, stamped his cunning high-topped shoes, glared up at her, until suddenly she'd turned from the sink and shouted back, "Oh, stop squeaking at me!" (pp. 95–96)

Mortified by such treatment, Scott finally relents and peddles his autobiography to a publisher. No sooner does "the first check for [Scott's] manuscript" (p. 144) arrive in the mail than Lou's attitude undergoes another transformation: "She'd told him how proud she was of him. She'd held his tiny hand and said, 'You're still the man I married, Scott'" (p. 144). Her renewed affection and respect, however, fail to restore Scott's sense of self-esteem. On the contrary, his feelings of emasculation and enslavement grow increasingly intense. The wedding band which he wears on a string around his neck becomes more than he can manage, a symbol of the impossibly heavy financial load he feels he must bear. Wearing it, Scott thinks, is "like carrying a great gold loop around" (p. 155). This sense of oppression becomes even more intense when, having shrunk to ten inches, he is forced to move into a "deluxe doll house," purchased with proceeds from his writing. This scale-model replica, complete with "fluffy white curtains," "a fireplace of false bricks," and nonfunctioning appliances (p. 154), is clearly a symbol of the larger (though no more substantial) suburban comforts that Scott has purchased for Lou at the cost of his manhood.

By the time Scott completes his autobiography ("Life in a Dollhouse" is the title of its final chapter), the allegorical implications of Matheson's story are impossible to ignore. Scott may feel like a freak—"homo reductus" (p. 130) is the name he invents for himself—but his story, though told in the "fantastically heightened" terms of horror fiction, is absolutely typical: a representative male fable of 1950s marriage. Each of the torments the tiny hero experiences—his captivity in a claustrophobic "dollhouse"; his hopeless struggle to satisfy his wife's insistent material desires; his inexorable transformation from a six-foot ex-soldier into a "ludicrous" man-baby (p. 33), an infantryman into an infant—is simply the nightmarish realization of extremely common postwar male anxieties. Even the scene in which Scott is set upon and battered about by the family cat corresponds to the common vulgarism for a man's subjugation by a domineering woman. Scott is both literally and figuratively "pussy-whipped."

The central symbol of Scott's conjugal anxiety, however, is neither the doll house nor the cat but the monstrous spider that serves as Scott's *bête noire* throughout the novel and that clearly embodies the hero's perception of his wife. Discussing Matheson's book in *Danse Macabre*, Stephen King (who is given to taking cheap shots at psychoanalysis even while availing himself of its insights) scoffs at critics who, to his way of thinking, make too much of the spider's meaning. King was at a party in the fall of 1978, he recounts, when a well-known woman science fiction writer offered the following theory: "In symbolic terms, this woman said, spiders represent the vagina.

The Incredible Shrinking Man *(1957) (Universal). Reprinted by permission.*

Scott finally kills his Nemesis . . . by impaling it on a pin (the phallic symbol, get it, get it?)." "All of this was well-meaning bullshit," King concludes, "but bullshit is still bullshit . . ."[49]

Though King's impatience with "half-baked Freudians" is hard to fault, the symbolic relation between women and spiders has, in fact, been widely documented not only by psychoanalytic critics but by students of world folklore as well. [50] Still, it's not necessary to invoke depth psychology or myth scholarship to establish a connection between Lou and the spider, since the text itself points quite clearly to such a reading, not only by making the spider a black widow[51]—"Men called it that," Scott muses, "because the female destroyed and ate the male" (p. 16)—but in other ways, too. Scott himself is aware that the spider represents something larger and describes it in highly suggestive terms: "The spider had come to symbolize something to him; something he hated, something he couldn't coexist with" (p. 157). "It was more than a spider. . . . It was every anxiety, insecurity, and fear in his life given a hideous night-black form" (p. 148). In short, Scott perceives the spider as a monstrous, man-eating female that is the source of all his anxieties and with whom he cannot coexist.

Equally significant is a remark Scott makes early on in the book, when he and Lou are embroiled in one of their frequent disputes over money:

> "I'm tired of being tested," he went on, not wanting to sink into the comfortless isolation of silence again. "I'm tired of basal-metabolism tests and protein-bound tests; tired of drinking radioactive iodine and barium-powdered water. . . . And what the hell's the point? They haven't found a thing. Not a *thing!* And they never will. And I can't see owing them thousands of dollars for nothing! . . ."
>
> "They weren't finished, Scott."
>
> "The bills don't matter to you," he said.
>
> "*You* matter to me," she answered.
>
> "And who's the 'security' bug in this marriage, anyway?" he asked.
>
> "That's not fair."
>
> "Isn't it? What brought us here from California in the first place? Me? Because I decided I just had to go into

business with Marty? I was happy out there. I didn't—" He drew in a shaking breath and let it empty from his lungs. (pp. 14—15)

Scott's metaphor is revealing. In his eyes, his wife is a "'security' bug." It's a striking image, explicitly associating the cannibalistic insect with Louise and her all-consuming hunger for middle-class suburban status. Though Stephen King is right to reject a reductively Freudian reading of Scott's situation, there seems little doubt that the shrinking man's conflict with the spider represents a battle of the sexes. Scott's struggle to vanquish the black widow represents his effort to free himself from the clutches of a devouring female creature whose only purpose, as far as he is concerned, is to snare him in a web and keep him trapped there forever as a permanent source of sustenance.

The same association between women and insects is made in what is certainly the most remarkable scene in the novel—an episode with no equivalent in the film. Scott, forty-two inches tall and stranded on a highway, is given a lift by a tipsy middle-aged man—a pederast, as it turns out, who takes Scott for a twelve-year-old and attempts to seduce him. During the drive, this aging homosexual, who is returning from dinner with a married friend named Vincent, launches into a vicious denunciation of "the hair shirt of matrimony" (p. 55). Wedlock, according to the driver, has reduced his friend to a pitiable state: "What was a *man*, dear boy, became, you see, a creature of degradation, a lackey, a serf, an automaton. A . . . lost shriveled soul" (pp. 55—56). He likens women "to cancer" (p. 57) and describes the experience of "meet[ing] your first woman" as "analogous to turning over your first rock and finding your first bug" (p. 56). What is so striking about this speech—besides its nastiness—is how neatly it summarizes the central issues of the story. Scott, too, perceives his wife as a "bug" and himself as the victim of an insidious condition which has reduced him to a "creature of degradation," a "shriveled soul." (Reflecting on the inability of his doctors to come up with a cure, Scott remarks bitterly, "Here I sit, shrivelling away, while they fumble" [p. 111].) In short, though the pederast is presented as a despicable, somewhat menacing character, the book does nothing to refute his point of view. On the contrary, the entire story can be seen, in effect, as the fantastic literalization of this character's misogynist metaphors.

Though the 1621 *History of Tom Thumbe* breaks off midway through the hero's adventures, a later and better-known version carries the story up to his death. Interestingly, Tom is slain by a giant spider:

> The king received Tom . . . into favor, which he did not live to enjoy, for a large spider one day attacked him; and although he drew his sword and fought well, yet the spider's poisonous breath at last overcame him.

> "He fell dead on the ground where he stood,
> And the spider sucked every drop of his blood."

Tom Thumb and the spider. Illustration by Arthur Rackham from Flora Annie Steel, English Fairy Tales *(1918).*

King Thunstone and his whole court were so sorry at the loss of their little favourite, that they went into mourning, and raised a fine white marble monument over his grave, with the following epitaph:

"Here lyes Tom Thumb, King Arthur's knight,
Who died by a spider's cruel bite.
He was well known in Arthur's court,
Where he afforded gallant sport;
He rode at tilt and tournament
And on a mouse a-hunting went.
Alive he filled the court with mirth;
His death to sorrow soon gave birth.
Wipe, wipe your eyes, and shake your head
And cry,—Alas! Tom Thumb is dead!"[52]

Reflecting a very different cultural mythology, Matheson's modern-day American version of "Tom Thumb" ends on a triumphant note, with the hero vanquishing his nemesis—the symbol of the feminizing forces that seek to housebreak and enslave him—and experiencing a profound sense of renewal. In the film, this rebirth takes the form of a quasi-religious experience—Scott's realization of his at-one-ment with the divine All. The book concludes with an even more characteristically American fantasy. Scott, shrunken now to microscopic size, escapes from his house and discovers, not the nothingness he had feared, but a glorious "new world" (p. 188), a trackless wilderness stretching westward from the walls of his domestic prison. He stands for a moment, relishing his freedom and contemplating the splendors of the new frontier—"its vivid splashes of vegetation, its scintillant hills, its towering trees, its sky of shifting hues" (p. 188). Then, like countless American folk heroes before him, he lights out for the territories.

4 | The Killer Granny

Archetypes of Schlock

A natural offspring of America's industrialized democracy, the tabloid has learned to time its beat with the pulse of the common people. With an exaggeration shared by all the national forms of expression, it recounts each day the folklore of our times.

—Simon Michael Bessie,
  Jazz Journalism

Of the many categories of popular art, the one which most closely resembles pure folklore is, as I've suggested, the type with the fewest socially or aesthetically redeeming values; that is, the type that both its detractors and admirers tend to refer to as pure schlock. Works that fall into this category—from funny animal comic books to Grade-Z exploitation movies to the kind of he-man adventure fiction found on the paperback racks of drugstores and Greyhound bus depots everywhere—make up the bulk of American popular art, for obvious reasons. After all, in the time it takes a comparatively serious pop writer—Joseph Wambaugh, for example, or Leon Uris—to produce a single blockbuster novel, an unabashed hack like Mickey Spillane can crank out enough bestsellers to fill an entire display case at Dalton's; and for every artsy horror movie like *The Shining* there are two *Doctor Butchers*, three *Creature from the Black Lagoons*, and four *Friday the Thirteenths*.

The rate at which such pop entertainments are created, of course, is one of the reasons they end up with the impersonal quality of folk tales, since it's hard (if not actively self-defeating) to worry about matters of style or personal expression when you have a deadline of three weeks to turn out a finished novel, sixty-four pages of comic book art, or a feature-length slasher movie. As a result, the majority of American pop artists have always seemed (or been) as anonymous as the nameless storytellers of folk tradition. Steven Spielberg may be as close to a household name as any Hollywood director is likely to get, but the creators of the Saturday-matinee serials and fifties B-movies that shaped his sensibility (pictures like *Spy Smashers*, *Revenge of the Creature*, *The Man from Planet X*, etc.) are unknown to everyone but the most devoted buffs. The book jackets of the phenomenally popular *Executioner* novels (an ongoing series which clearly comes out of a book factory and which follows the exploits of a cleancut, all-American commando named

Mack Bolan as he does battle with Commie miscreants across the globe) don't even bother to list an author anymore. Indeed, in those instances when a pop artist working within an entertainment mill does bring a distinctive style to his work (as, for example, Disney artist Carl Barks did in the Donald Duck comics he produced for twenty years, beginning in the mid-1940s) he is recognized as such a rarity that he is likely to find himself hailed as a genius, with scholarly monographs and lavishly illustrated coffee table books devoted to his art.

But turning out successful pop art—i.e., stuff that sells—at a breakneck speed requires more than a kind of totally nondescript technical skill. More importantly, it requires creators distinguished (as Leslie Fiedler puts it) by "easy access to their own unconscious where it impinges on the collective unconscious of their time";[1] in effect, people with a talent for dreaming up the very fantasies that the mass audience (with or without being aware of it) craves, at a given moment, to hear or read or see. But these fantasies (inevitably, given the constants of human nature) turn out to be precisely those stories which have always amazed, amused, titillated, or terrified listeners, reinvented (mostly unself-consciously, though at times quite knowingly) in forms that relate to whatever anxieties or fads or obsessions happen to be in the air: stories, in short, with both the function and essential form of traditional folk tales.

That schlock entertainment—what Fiedler calls "commodity art"[2]—has always dealt with the same, essentially folkloric themes can be confirmed by a look at one of the most popular nineteenth-century publications, the *Illustrated Police News* of London, a weekly tabloid with "the largest circulation of any periodical of its time."[3] This wildly sensationalistic paper—which makes contemporary counterparts like the *Weekly World News* seem like *Partisan Review*—specialized in graphically illustrated stories of atrocious murders, bizarre accidents, spectacular natural disasters, and the more ingenious and colorful

The shameless combination of pornography and piety embodied in this engraving is typical of the tabloid style. From the Illustrated Police News.

forms of suicide (self-crucifixions were especially popular), all vividly recounted in the pious, tongue-clucking tone that has always been the sleazemonger's favorite ploy and accompanied by equally lurid and lovingly detailed engravings.

To be sure, many of these articles were nothing more than the journalistic equivalent of public executions, which were, in fact, another staple of the *Illustrated Police News*. The frontispiece of Leonard DeVries' book, *'Orrible Murder*, a collection of pieces from this Victorian crime-and-scandal sheet, is a full-page illustration of a particularly juicy hanging in which the force of the fall has ripped off the prisoner's head; his body, meanwhile, continues to drop through the air with its hands clasped in a prayerlike gesture of last-minute repentance and a geyser of blood spurting out its neck. (The image of the headless corpse plunging to the ground in an attitude of contrition perfectly captures the paper's shamelessly hypocritical style, its method of serving up hardcore violence under the pretext of moral improvement.) DeVries' book is full of features with catchy titles like "Singular Method of Execution," "Lynching Four Men," and (my personal favorite) "Capital Punishments of All Nations," another highly educational article illustrating ways people have been tortured and put to death throughout history. ("Beheading was a military punishment among the Romans. The head of the culprit was laid on a block placed in a pit dug for the purpose beyond the *Vallum* and preparatory to the stroke he was tied to a stake and whipped with cords . . .")[4]

The brutal mistreatment of women and children (the flip side of the official Victorian myth of domestic beatitude, the fantasy Fiedler calls "Home as Heaven")[5] also received regular, not to say obsessive, attention in the pages of the *Illustrated Police News*. Though the paper did take note of an occasional atrocity committed by women against men (a wife who set her husband on fire by hurling a lamp at him during a domestic quarrel; a girl who doused her sleeping stepfather with boiling water

THE WHITECHAPEL TRAGEDY

Victorian splatter: a typically gruesome murder from the Illustrated Police News.

"and when he awoke attacked him with a red hot bar of iron"), such stories were far outnumbered by accounts of "shocking cruelty" to children (beatings, stabbings, stompings, and worse) and—even more common—savage attacks on women. "Frightful Wife Murder in Bristol," "Young Woman Decapitated," "Fearful Scene—Woman Torn to Pieces," "Throwing a Wife Out of the Window," "Murderous Attack on a Woman in Whitney," "Extraordinary Wife Murder," "Murder and Mutilation of a Woman"—these are just a small sample of the articles reprinted by DeVries along with their accompanying illustrations, many of which (an enraged husband slitting his wife's throat with a straight razor; the police uncovering a sack full of butchered female body parts) are seriously unsettling, even in this era of the slasher, slice 'n' dice, and splatter film. Indeed, one consolation to be derived from DeVries' book is that it demonstrates what he calls the "unchanging social taste" for such spectacle and makes it clear that the only thing new about modern sex-and-sadism movies—cinematic gorefests like *Bloodthirsty Butchers*, *Meatcleaver Massacre*, and *I Eat Your Skin*—is the technology involved in producing them. If these films prove anything at all, it is not that our taste or morals have degenerated but simply that popular techniques for simulating violence have come a long way since the wood engraving.

More significantly, DeVries' book confirms that pop works aimed at the general public have always been, in essence, a form of mass-produced folklore. The brand of horror-porn sadism peddled by the *Illustrated Police News* is itself a fundamental part of folk tradition, as Erwin Panofsky suggests in his famous essay "Style and Medium in the Motion Pictures," where he identifies the five "most important . . . elements" of all folk entertainments (including film) as sentimentality, moral justice, crude humor, mild pornography, and sadism. [6]

But the *Illustrated Police News* is by no means entirely or even primarily given over to gore, to the gratification of what Panofsky calls the "primordial instinct for bloodshed and cruelty." [7] Even a glance at the paper's favorite (and highly overworked) adjectives—"extraordinary," "singular," "incredible," "thrilling," "miraculous"—reveals that the primary emotion it aims to evoke is not horror, revulsion, or morbid fascination but pure wonder. Though the writers often insist that they are reporting the strict (if admittedly remarkable) truth, many of the stories clearly owe more to folklore than fact. More than anything else, DeVries' anthology seems like an illustrated col-

The pages of the tabloids are heavily populated with creatures out of folklore and legend. From the Illustrated Police News.

lection of wondertales: of stories about sea monsters ("Fearful Encounter with a Sea Devil"), living skeletons ("A Burglar Bitten by a Skeleton"), hidden rooms or mysterious trunks full of human remains ("A Horrible Discovery"), people who accidentally swallow loathsome creatures that continue to live inside their bodies ("Death from Swallowing a Mouse"), and other marvels.[8] Indeed, many of the stories compiled by DeVries could easily be cataloged under the motif headings used by folklore scholars: the Corpse Chamber, the Return of the Dead, the Revenant as Skeleton, Dreadful Contaminations, etc.

At the same time, the engravings which illustrate the stories bear a striking resemblance to scenes from popular movies: a drawing of a young man being "snapped in two by . . . a monstrous shark" might have come straight out of *Jaws*; another, showing some workmen breaking into a sealed-off room in an old house and discovering the skeletal corpse of an old woman "seated in an antique chair," looks remarkably like the climax of *Psycho*,[9] and so on. In the end, the reader of DeVries' book comes away from it with a sense not so much of humanity's unquenchable appetite for blood and gore as for our unceasing fascination with the same set of bizarre and astounding tales.

In one sense, however, folk stories (which, far from being the relics of a preliterate past, continue to lead a vigorous existence, as the work of Jan Harold Brunvand makes clear) never remain absolutely the same, since they are always appearing in new and up-to-date forms that reflect the cultural concerns of the moment. The urban belief tale that supplies the title for Brunvand's second collection, *The Choking Doberman*, is a case in point. This story, which spread rapidly across the United States in 1981 (I recall hearing it at about that time from a neighbor, who insisted that it had actually happened to someone living a few blocks away), involves a woman who returns home from a shopping expedition to find her pet Doberman gagging violently. She rushes the animal to a vet, who extracts three human fingers from the dog's throat. The police are called,

TERRIBLE·DISCOVERY·OF·A·SKELETON

Though the technology for transmitting them has changed, the fantasies portrayed by pop art have remained remarkably constant. This engraving from the Illustrated Police News *is strikingly similar to the climax of Hitchcock's* Psycho.

they search the woman's house, and—hearing whimpers and moans coming from the bedroom closet—open it to discover the wounded, would-be burglar, cowering in a corner in a state of shock.

In trying to locate the folkloric roots of this apparently present-day story, Brunvand traces a complicated (though thoroughly convincing) genealogy, which includes early Celtic legends about helpful animals, "rural witchcraft lore in which a supernatural intruder . . . is severely injured, often in hand or fingers," and a variety of other common folk motifs, such as "The Thief Who Had His Hand Cut Off."[10] In so doing, Brunvand vividly demonstrates not only how traditional folk stories are constantly being revised and updated but also how they serve as an extremely reliable index of a community's current preoccupations (so that "The Choking Doberman" turns out to be not a unique and unprecedented tale, and certainly not the report of a real-life incident, but a very old folk story refashioned for an age of urban crime).

Brunvand concludes his successful search for the folklore antecedents of "The Choking Doberman" legend by quoting (with admitted, and perfectly justified, self-satisfaction) the nineteenth-century English folklorist Sabine Baring-Gould: "There is scarcely a story which I hear which I cannot connect with some family of myths."[11] If the same claim can be made in regard to many pop narratives—action/adventure comics, B-movies, and the like—it is because so much of this material consists of the same story types and motifs as the more traditional kinds of folklore studied by people like Baring-Gould and Brunvand. To see Wes Craven's film *The Hills Have Eyes* (a brutal little shocker about an all-American family on a cross-country trip who run afoul of a clan of mutant, cannibalistic hill people) in the context of such feral-family legends as those concerning Sawney Beane, or to see Oliver Stone's psychological horror movie *The Hand* (in which Michael Caine plays an artist whose marriage is falling apart and whose right hand, chopped off in a traffic accident, returns to take revenge on the people who have betrayed him) as a film in which modern-day divorce anxieties are assimilated to the folk-motif known as the Revenant as Hand[12]—to make these connections brings us closer to the meaning not only of these particular films but of pop art in general.

I think it's safe to say that the desire to perpetuate an age-old narrative tradition is the furthest thing from the minds of most, if not all, pop storytellers (pulp novelists, schlock film-makers, etc.), the vast majority of whom are undoubtedly only in it for the money. But the point is that to achieve that (perfectly legitimate) goal, they have to find and deliver the stories that will sell. To a large extent, this means keeping a close eye on the current (and constantly changing) interests of the mass audience. But it also means embodying those interests in stories with the most basic and persistent appeal. As a result, the unpretentious, purely commercial-minded pop craftsman often finds himself, willy-nilly, turning out the contemporary versions of traditional folktales, for if (with the calculation of the hack) he is adept at exploiting the news he is also (with the instinct of the born storyteller) highly skilled at hitting upon those themes and motifs which never seem to grow old.

The schlockmeister's genius for packaging his audience's latest preoccupations in stories of ancient and universal appeal is nowhere more apparent than in the supermarket tabloid, the most cheerfully exploitive—and purely folkloric—form of contemporary subliterature. These weekly publications—the modern American heirs of the *Illustrated Police News*—present themselves as genuinely journalistic enterprises, pulp versions of *Newsweek* and *Time*, gathering together, from the four corners of the globe, stories too sensational for their more respectable cousins to cover: "all the news that isn't fit to print," in the words of one particularly censorious critic. [13] Even a cursory glance at their contents, however, reveals that, if they report on anything at all, it is not the state of the world but the state of mind of the American "underculture" (to use Richard Dorson's term). Each issue is a modern-day folk miscellany, a fifty-page collection of tall tales, fables, and wonder stories tricked out and peddled as truth.

Partly because of the extreme tawdriness of these papers, their carnival (not to say freakshow) flavor, and partly because many respectable folk scholars remain fixed in their distaste for "commodity art," which they see as inimical to the health, indeed the very survival, of authentic folk culture, no folklorist that I know of has made an in-depth study of the supermarket tabloid. But scholars who see the mass media as utterly destructive of American folk tradition clearly do not spend enough time at their local Grand Union or A & P, browsing through the reading matter at the checkout counter racks. If they did, they would discover a treasure trove of legend and lore as rich (in its own tacky way) as material collected from more traditional sources. In terms of what it can tell us about flourishing American folk beliefs, a single issue of the *Weekly World News* is surely as valuable as, say, a field trip to the Blue Ridge Mountains or the ethnic ghettos of Baltimore.

This is not to say that the folkloric quality of the tabloids has gone completely unnoted. Indeed, newspapers in general have long been recognized by certain scholars and media critics as an important mode of modern-day "legend-transmission." [14] Linda Dégh, for example, who has done more, perhaps, than any other folklorist to call her colleagues' attention to the "interaction of folklore and mass media," observes that "in countless cases it is beyond doubt that the newspaper . . . [has been] instrumental in the creation of a new legend, as well as in the revitalization, modification, dissemination, and maintenance of an old legend." [15] Dégh's point is amply—indeed massively—

documented in an engagingly quirky collection, *Superstition and the Press*, assembled by a journalist named Curtis D. Mac-Dougall. Drawn entirely from mainstream papers such as the *Los Angeles Times*, the *Philadelphia Inquirer*, the *Washington Post*, and the *Chicago Daily News*, MacDougall's bulky volume compiles a decade's worth of stories on a score of popular subjects: Astrology, Prophecy, Spiritualism, Exorcism, Poltergeists, Psychic Healing, Sea Serpents, Witchcraft, Religious Miracles, Clairvoyance, UFOs, and more. [16] The sheer size of the book—over six hundred densely packed pages of clippings—is striking confirmation of the heavily folkloric emphasis of the modern newspaper, its resemblance (in Marshall McCluhan's words) to "an Arabian Night's entertainment in which a thousand and one astonishing tales are . . . told by an anonymous narrator to an anonymous audience." [17]

What is true for respectable papers is (as McCluhan also notes) doubly so for their "more sensational" cousins, [18] a fact recognized as far back as 1938 by Simon Michael Bessie, whose bright, lively study, *Jazz Journalism*, treats the tabloids as a uniquely modern form of folklore. "Embalmed in their arresting pictures and bold headlines," Bessie writes, "are the happenings and persons that comprise the folklore of our times, more so than in the conventional newspaper because from the start the tabloid identified itself with the common people." [19] Bessie himself sees the difference between respectable papers and tabloids more as a matter of style than of substance, and MacDougall's enormous assemblage of news items on fantastical subjects would certainly seem to bear him out. Still, that difference is crucial. While papers like the *Chicago Sun-Times* and the *Minneapolis Tribune* may indeed devote a surprising amount of space to stories about Sasquatch, the Lake Champlain sea monster, and the Curse of Cahuenga, they tend to approach these topics in an openly skeptical spirit. Thus, when a University of Chicago biologist named Roy P. Mackal undertook a trip to the jungles of Zaire in 1981 to search for the legendary Mokele-Mbembe (a long-necked, fifteen-ton lizard said to be the last surviving member of a dinosaurlike species), newspapers throughout the country covered the story extensively but in a highly incredulous, even satirical, tone. (One column in the *New York Daily News*, for example, was headlined "Move Over, Don Quixote.")[20] For the most part, while conventional newspapers are only too ready to run stories on Bigfoot sightings, UFO landings, psychic healings, and the like ("newspapers live on legends," according to Dégh and Vázsonyi),[21] they generally see these phenomena either as examples of profound gullibility—of the deplorable persistence of primitive superstition in an age of science and reason—or, more sympathetically (though only slightly less condescendingly), as the sign of a touching human capacity for wonder and belief.

Publications like the *Weekly World News*, the *National Examiner*, and the *Sun*, on the other hand, are in the business of catering to, not exposing, the credulity of the "common people." In the world of the supermarket tabloid, no story is too far-fetched or outrageous to be served up as absolute fact. Unlike legitimate newspapers, the tabloids do not exist to investigate wild rumors and weird beliefs but, on the contrary, to perpetuate (indeed, often to generate) them. They disseminate the most brazen fabulations in a tone of devout, even urgent, sincerity, very much in the manner of a neighborhood gossip swearing to the honest-to-God truth of some (clearly apocryphal) incident. For this reason, it is possible to regard the supermarket tabloid not as a supremely sleazy kind of newspaper—the black sheep of the journalistic family—but as the mass-produced, printed equivalent of the so-called foaf: the mythical "friend-of-a-friend" who is commonly invoked in oral, urban legendry as the unimpeachable source of the story (as in, "This really happened to a friend-of-a-friend of mine").[22] The journalistic trappings of the tabloid—the headlines, bylines, columns, features, and so forth—exist solely to create an illusion of authority, conferring instant (if totally spurious) validity on its contents. By presenting the most hoary fantasies—marvels and miracles, portents and prodigies—in a newspaper format, the supermarket tabloid performs one of the essential functions of the traditional folk raconteur: the re-creation of archetypal narratives in the most up-to-the-minute forms. Paul Dickson and Joseph C. Goulden, collectors of American "credos" ("widely held beliefs" that are "partially, predominantly, or totally wrong"), make a similar point when they describe the supermarket tabloid as the twentieth-century "equivalent of marketplace babble."[23]

But if tabloid writers possess a genuine gift for working endless variations on a limited number of very old themes, for modernizing (and Americanizing) stories known in all times and places, they are equally adept at the opposite; that is, describing real-life occurrences in fantastical terms. On those occasions when a true and verifiable story does make it into the *Weekly World News,* for example, it is invariably reported in the language of myth and folklore. Thus, an article about a woman's efforts to locate the anonymous M.D. who came to the aid of her injured husband following a Florida freeway accident is headlined, "LOVING WIFE'S SEARCH FOR PHANTOM PHYSICIAN" (August 26, 1986, p. 4)—a caption which places a fairly mundane news item in the context of a popular folktale category, formally known as "Ghost Aids Living in Emergency" (Motif E 363.1). Similarly, a rather sorry tale about a destitute woman who found an envelope crammed with cash and, believing it to be a gift from St. Jude, proceeded to pay off her debts (only to be arrested and charged with larceny) is trumpeted in the *Weekly World News* as an instance of divine intervention: "$$ FROM HEAVEN: POOR MOM'S PRAYER MIRACULOUSLY ANSWERED" (September 3, 1985, p. 7). Indeed, one interesting side-effect of long-term exposure to these papers, I learned, is a growing tendency to translate legitimate news items into tabloidese, so that, for example, it becomes hard to read a piece in the *New York Times* on the discovery of Gigantopithecus—a prehistoric race of colossal primates whose fossil remains have recently turned up in Southeast Asia[24]—without instantly perceiving it as folklore: "KING KONG LIVED!" or "BONES OF ANCIENT BIGFOOT TRIBE DISCOVERED BY SCIENTISTS!"

I acquired this particular habit of mind between September 24, 1985, and September 30, 1986, the year I spent as a subscriber to two popular (and highly sensationalistic) publications, the *Sun* and the *Weekly World News*. The *National Enquirer*—the best-known and most widely distributed of the tabloids—certainly isn't without anthropological interest, as Fred E. H. Schroeder makes clear in a provocative piece on the *Enquirer* as a cultural "fetish" object.[25] Still, this venerable rag, which chronicles, with lip-smacking gusto, the missteps and mortifications of the rich and fleetingly famous ("CHRISTINA DELOREAN REVEALS HER SECRET AGONY!"), has grown comparatively mundane since its old "MOM CHOPS UP BABY AND STUFFS IT IN GARBAGE PAIL" days. Indeed, with its four-color photos and glossy paper, the *Enquirer* has become positively slick. Happily for aficionados of schlock, the reportorial traditions (and intensely cheesy look) of the old, precolor *Enquirer* continue to live on in the *Weekly World News*, which not only retains the unsavory appearance of its infamous forebear (indeed, the *News* was started up to utilize— and continues to be printed on—the *Enquirer*'s old black-and-white press) but also specializes in the sort of outlandish belief tales that made the *Enquirer* such a lively and intriguing read before it metamorphosed into a Hollywood scandal sheet.

The *Sun* is, if anything, an even more disreputable example of the genre—a supermarket tabloid which traffics more-or-less entirely in the make-believe. Indeed, it is this complete devotion to the extravagantly implausible that makes the *Sun* so fascinating from a folkloric point of view. My attention was first drawn to this tabloid as I waited in a grocery-store checkout line several years ago and contemplated the front-page photo of its then-current issue: a sickly, green-tinted shot of what was clearly an outraged rhesus monkey with pointy, Mr. Spock ears affixed to its head. "UFO ALIEN WITH PIRANHA TEETH ATTACKS SCIENTIST!" blared the accompanying caption. The other headlines plastered across page one were equally fantastic, dispatches from the dreamworld of legend and myth: "MERMAIDS KEEP MAN TWO YEARS AS LOVE SLAVE," "GHOST IN LOVE WITH GROOM CHASES BRIDE OUT OF THE HOUSE," "RUSSIANS CLONE WILD CAVEMAN FOUND IN SIBERIA," "SHE COMES BACK FROM THE DEAD AFTER 42 YEARS," "PREGNANT MAN GIVES BIRTH."

In *Class,* his entertaining "guide through the American status system," Paul Fussell describes the supermarket tabloids as "prole weeklies,"[26] and, indeed, it seems safe to assume that the *Sun* appeals to a very different constituency from that of, say, the *New York Review of Books*—that its regular readers are, by and large, people of distinctly narrow means and limited education. Interestingly (and somewhat unaccountably), however, the *Weekly World News* has recently enjoyed a kind of mini-vogue among the intelligentsia. David Byrne, for example (the thinking man's rock star and all-around multi-media prodigy), is a self-declared enthusiast: his critically acclaimed 1986 movie *True Stories* (a kind of New Wave *Our Town*) was largely inspired by articles from the tabloid. The *Weekly World News* (in transparent disguise) is even more central to Francine Prose's marvelous 1986 novel *Bigfoot Dreams,* whose heroine, Vera Perl, is a staff writer for the paper (pseudonymously called *This Week*). For much of the book, Vera is afflicted with serious doubts about her work. She has so thoroughly assimilated the viewpoint of the tabloid that everything in the world (her own

PSYCHIC HEALER WAKES COMA BOY

'The patient was brain dead . . . it's incredible,' say doctors

WEEKLY WORLD 55¢

NEWS

VAMPIRE HOTEL
You can check in — but you might not check out!

June 10, 1986   30587   VOL. 7, Issue 35

INCREDIBLE PHOTOS OF AMAZING INFANT

TWO-HEADED BABY IS DOING GREAT!

One face smiles while the other cries, say astounded doctors

Wealthy mom who killed her kids set free after 20 months

'My perfect hubby is a pain,' wife tells divorce court

Hungry crocodile eats bird watcher

America's biggest and brightest horoscope!

BABY FACTORY!
Wondermom has 9 kids in 6 years — and she loves it

DISASTROUS GIFT!
'Power to predict earthquakes ruined my life,' says mom

Stupid dog gobbles up $480 cash in stunned vet's office

Folklore masquerading as fact: the Weekly World News.
Reprinted by permission.

life included) has taken on its crackpot coloring; indeed, she can't even experience a simple bout of depression without immediately transforming it into a frenzied headline ("WOMAN SITS IN SAME CHAIR THIRTY YEARS!"). Even more dispiriting is her growing sense of guilt over what she sees as the paper's cynical exploitation of its audience's anxieties and woes (to say nothing of their gullibility).

What saves Vera in the end is a kind of epiphany, a perception of the tabloid as a benign, even inspirational, work—evidence of humanity's infinite capacity for hope, its quenchless faith in the possibilities of self-renewal. The insight hits her as she contemplates the (completely fictitious) account of a "healthy 8-pound-12-ounce baby boy" born to a (nonexistent) ninety-one-year-old named Sara Beckley:

> Moved by the realization that 91-YEAR-OLD MOM BEARS BOUNCING BABE is the quintessential *This Week* story, Vera's filled with more love for this shoddy, sensationalist rag than she could possibly say. There's nothing but hope in this story, hope and goodwill: hope for all the women who want children and can't have them, for women like Vera who already have a child and regret that they probably won't have more. Ninety-one! There's still time! False hope—but what's the harm? . . . Between the lines of this story is everyone's longing for miracles, the hope that goes against all odds, beyond synchronicity and breaks in the natural order. The promise that your suffering leads to heaven and the cafeteria of your dreams, your forty years in the wilderness to glades of milk and honey. . . . Only now—how slow she is!—does Vera realize that Sara Beckley laughing at her newborn son is Sarah in the Bible.[27]

Prose's perception of the cheering and reassuring nature of the tabloid is confirmed by other commentators as well. Paul

Fussell, for example, writes that "the essential function of the prole weeklies is to soothe and comfort,"[28] while Fred E. H. Schroeder, referring to the *Enquirer*, speaks of its "weekly promises of salvation and weekly hopes of deliverance from troubles and mortality."[29] And there is a good deal of truth to this claim. The fact is, however, that the peddling of hope is the business of many mass publications. Indeed, popular magazines in general—from *Cosmopolitan* to *Money* to *Runner's World*—are packed with redemptive promises, conjuring up consoling visions of a better life and a brighter future and offering quasi-magical formulas (involving talismanic catchwords like "expert" and "specialist") to achieve rebirth and salvation. Indeed, one major difference between publications like the *Weekly World News* and, say, *Esquire* is that, for all its insubstantiality, the tabloid is, in a strange sort of way, beyond trendiness, less subject to the whims of fashion. Though it's hard to imagine a more ephemeral piece of printed matter than the *Weekly World News* (which, with its cheesy paper and shoddy printing, seems to be manufactured with the garbage can in mind), there is a peculiarly timeless quality to the supermarket tabloid. Contemplating the contents of the "rag" she writes for, Prose's heroine Vera thinks, "Its ageless plots could have come from the ancient Greeks."[30] And, in fact, what gives the supermarket tabloid its special flavor is precisely this outlandish amalgam of the eternal and the trivial, the miraculous and utterly mundane: Abraham's wife, Sarah, reincarnated as Mrs. Albert Beckley of Chicago, Illinois.

There is no doubt that, as Prose suggests, the tabloids draw on the Bible (particularly the Old Testament) for inspiration. The December 10, 1985, issue of the *Weekly World News*, for example, features a story headlined "TREASURE HUNTERS FIND NOAH'S ARK," while "MIDGET WHIPS TOWN BULLY" (*WWN*, February 6, 1986) is clearly a reworking of the David and Goliath story. Still, pagan belief and primitive folklore are far more common in the tabloid than Judeo-Christian mythology. "One cannot help but believe," writes Fred E. H. Schroeder, "that many readers of [the *Enquirer*] are religious—the tone is so close to that of Christian radio and television." Nevertheless, he points out, "institutional religion" gets decidedly "short shrift" in the tabloid, while "primitivism runs rampant."[31]

My own taxonomical study of the tabloids, conducted over the course of a year, bears Schroeder out. The majority of articles in the *Weekly World News* and the *Sun*, I found, fall into a relatively limited number of distinct folktale categories. To be sure, there are various unclassifiable tales. As far as I can determine, Thompson's index offers no analogues to "STORE OWNER BEATEN UP WITH FOOT-LONG CHILI DOG," for instance, or "TOWN TERRORIZED BY GIANT DUCK."[32] Other stories embody a set of recurrent fantasies and themes that appear to be indigenous to the tabloid. For the most part, however, the contents of these papers are updated, unmistakably American variants of narrative motifs well-known throughout the world. The following survey of these motifs—as well as of those archetypes (or, perhaps more properly, schlocktypes) peculiar to the tabloid—isn't meant to be definitive. But it will, I trust, help to establish the essentially folkloric character of these publications—these crudely made collections of weird beliefs, old wives' tales, and whoppers—and shed some light on the preoccupying concerns of their audience.

When, at the very start of *Bigfoot Dreams*, Vera Perl reflects on the drawbacks of her job, particularly on the stultifying effect of concocting the same kinds of stories over and over, she offers a quick summary of the tabloid's pet topics: "UFO sightings, sex-change aliens, cancer cures in the humblest garden vegetables, new evidence of life after death. Yetis, Loch Ness monsters, live dinosaurs in hidden African valleys."[33] These and similar tabloid favorites are, of course, simply pseudo-scientific versions of common folk-themes. When the *Sun*, for example, prints a story about the capture of an "adolescent Bigfoot" ("BIGFOOT CAUGHT BY 5 HUNTERS," October 15, 1985), it scrupulously cites "renowned Bigfootologist, Cameron Allen," who testifies to the subject's height, weight, and blood-type. The fact is, however, that the ever-popular Bigfoot is a pure figment of the folk imagination, an all-American version of the mythic creature known as the Wild Man (*Homo ferus*), who has prowled the dreams of Western society throughout the centuries. [34]

The *Sun* and the *Weekly World News* are full of such refurbished folk stories: Miracle cures made of men's toiletries ("AFTERSHAVE LOTION CAN BRING PEOPLE BACK FROM DEATH," *Sun*, February 4, 1986), haunted high-tech equipment ("COMPUTER POSSESSED BY THE DEVIL TERRORIZES BOY," *Sun*, November 19, 1985), vampires afflicted with AIDS ("DRACULA WAS GAY," *WWN*, November 26, 1985), out-of-body encounters with celebrity spirits ("I WENT TO HEAVEN, MET ELVIS, AND TOOK HIS PHOTO AS PROOF," *Sun*, October 28, 1986), "space angels" responsible for miraculous conceptions ("I GAVE BIRTH TO A UFO BABY," *Sun*, August 27, 1985), mermaids wiped out by oil spills ("3 MERMAIDS FOUND KILLED BY POLLUTION," *WWN*, July 29, 1986). Clearly, one of the main functions of these mock-journalistic fairy tales is to transport their readers as far away as possible from their routine concerns—to provide them with a salutary dose of what the determinedly high-minded among us sneeringly call "escapism." Equally central to the supermarket tabloid, however, are those stories that focus precisely on the most fundamental conditions of its audience's day-to-day life.

Since that audience consists mostly of working-class housewives and mothers, two of its major concerns are, unsurprisingly, parenthood and marriage, a fact which accounts for the tabloids' high concentration of horror stories, tearjerkers, and wondertales concerning pregnancy, childbirth, offspring, and husbands (or "hubbies" as they are invariably called in the *Weekly World News* and the *Sun*). Though these pieces are presented in the same bizarre-but-true spirit as the curiosa collected by Robert Ripley, they are, for the most part, close (if characteristically tawdry) analogues of stories classified under section T ("Sex") of Stith Thompson's motif-index. Like all tabloid concoctions, in short (indeed, like low-grade American pop art in general), they deliver archetypal fantasy in the exuberantly vulgar tones of a carnival barker or a TV game show host, so that reading them can be weirdly disjunctive experience—a little like hearing one of Perrault's *contes du temps passé* recited by Monty Hall.

The headline story of the August 20, 1985, issue of the *Sun*—"UNBORN BABY KICKS BROTHER OUT OF WOMB"—is a prime example. "Two embryo brothers fought for survival in their mother's womb for two months before the stronger one kicked his brother out," the lead paragraph begins. "The surviving child grew and lived. The other baby died." The article is accompanied by a portrait of two beaming parents, "David and Louise Smith," proudly displaying their cuddly little fratricide. (Like the old *Illustrated Police News*, today's tabloids are highly pictorial, jam-packed with celebrity snapshots, cute-animal pictures, voyeuristic photos of accident victims and freaks, and artists' renditions of the more camera-shy subjects, like Bigfoot.) In spite of this documentary proof of the story's veracity, however, the article, as any folklorist would immediately recognize, is a precise embodiment of the motif known as "Twins Quarrel before Birth in Mother's Womb" (T 575.1.3). Since it seems doubtful that the average writer for the *Sun* relies on the *Motif-Index of Folk-Literature* as a reference tool, the likeliest explanation for this striking correspondence is simply that, like most successful producers of narrative schlock, tabloid writers possess an intuitive feel for those perennial fantasies that, for whatever reason, are irresistibly appealing to the imagination of "the folk."

My year-long study of the *Sun* and the *Weekly World News* turned up many other tabloid variants of traditional folk tales involving magical pregnancies and births. Motif T 584.2, for instance ("Child Removed from Body of Dead Mother"), was represented by various accounts of posthumous parturition, including "DROWNED GIRL GIVES BIRTH UNDERWATER" (*Sun*, February 4, 1986), "DEAD WOMAN BECOMES PREGNANT" (*Sun*, July 29, 1986), and "MOM RETURNS FROM THE GRAVE FOR A MIRACLE BIRTH" (*WWN*, September 24, 1985). A closely related article—and one that perfectly exemplifies the tabloid approach—is "COMA GIRL PREGNANT," a front-page story from the October 22, 1985, issue of the *Weekly World News*. In the world of the supermarket tabloid, comas invariably function as the modern-day equivalent of the folk-motif known as "Magic Sleep Extending over Many Years" (D 1960), of which the story of "Sleeping Beauty" is, perhaps, the best-known example. And, indeed, this article— about a twenty-four-year-old woman who, after being "left a helpless vegetable in an auto accident," was raped in the hospital by an unknown assailant—explicitly refers to the fairy tale ("Sleeping Beauty was victim of heartless attack," reads the subhead). This lurid reinvention of the childhood classic—in which the heroine isn't awakened by a kiss but sexually violated in her sleep—is an unmistakable product of what Panofsky calls the "folk-art mentality," which is compounded, in the main, of "plain sentimentality," "a primordial instinct for . . . cruelty," and "a taste for mild pornography."[35]

While fecund corpses and pregnant coma-girls are two of the tabloid's favorite fertility symbols, they are by no means the only ones. The pages of the *Sun* and the *Weekly World News* are densely populated with marvels of female procreative power, from "miracle moms" who give birth without ovaries (*Sun*, December 24, 1985) to human "baby factories" who manufacture children in record time ("AMAZING MOM GIVES BIRTH TWICE—IN SIX DAYS," *WWN*, July 29, 1986) or quantity ("SHE LOVES KIDS SO MUCH SHE'S HAD ONE A YEAR SINCE 1970," *WWN*, June 3, 1986). The great popularity of these stories—which correspond, respectively, to Motifs T 540 ("Miraculous Births") and T 586 ("Multiple Births")—is an accurate indication of the socioeconomic status of the typical tabloid reader, who belongs to that class of women more-or-less completely untouched by the modern feminist movement; that is, women whose lives remain firmly centered on maternal and domestic activities. For the most part, the "New Woman" is nowhere in sight in the *Sun* and the *Weekly World News*. The folk-heroes celebrated in their pages are women who have distinguished themselves, not in the fields of art, business, politics, or sports, but rather in the realm of reproduction. Magazines like *McCall's*, *Ladies Home Journal*, and *Woman's Day* might run paeans to Jeana Yeager, co-pilot of the *Voyager*, the first airplane to fly around the world on a single load of fuel. From the tabloid point of view, however, her achievement pales before that of "daring Michelle Einhorn," a pregnant twenty-two-year-old sky-diver who broke "all aviation records by making history's first mid-air delivery" ("WOMAN GIVES BIRTH WHILE PARACHUTING," *Sun*, October 29, 1985).

There is no folk-fantasy so wildly unbelievable that the tabloids will not print it and swear to its truth. If anything, the exaggerations of traditional folklore tend to be stretched even further in their tabloid incarnations. For example, while Thompson's motif-index lists several stories involving fantastically prolonged gestations (classified under the headings "Long Pregnancy: Twelve Months" [T 574.1] and "Long Pregnancy: Seven Years" [T 574.2]), the variant that appears in the November 12, 1985, issue of the *Sun* deals with a woman who carried a "hibernating fetus" in her womb for a full decade ("WOMAN PREGNANT 10 YEARS HAS BABY"). Similarly, though the folktales of anomalous newborns cataloged by Thompson under Motif T 550 ("Monstrous Births") are certainly fantastic enough, they seem almost restrained compared to the extravagance of their tabloid analogues. Thompson's index, for example, cites two stories—one from India, one Chinese—concerning women who give birth to a frog and a toad, respectively. By comparison, the February 18, 1986, issue of the *Sun* features a front-page story about a mother who bore, not just one reptile, but triplets ("WOMAN GIVES BIRTH TO 3 LIZARD BABIES WITH 12-INCH TAILS").

Folklore is full of women who produce subhuman offspring, often as the result of bestiality (Motif T554, "Woman Gives Birth to Animal"). Tabloid readers are regularly treated not only to the same titillating stories (e.g., "WOMAN GIVES BIRTH TO BLACK SHEEP," *Sun*, October 28, 1986) but to the opposite, and even more outlandish, fantasy as well—tales about beasts who beget human children (e.g., "CHIMP GIVES BIRTH TO HUMAN BABY," *Sun*, September 24, 1985). Of all newborn monstrosities, however, the runaway favorite among tabloid readers is incontestably the beloved two-headed baby. Under Motif T 551.2, "Child Born with Two Heads," Thompson cites a single African folk story. By contrast, in less than a four-month period, the *Weekly World News* alone published a half-dozen examples of this motif, with headlines like "TWO-HEADED BABY IS DOING GREAT" (June 10, 1986) and "TWO-HEADED BABY IS ALIVE AND KICKING" (April 1, 1986). The popularity of these "bizarre tots" (as they are commonly referred to) isn't hard to explain. For one thing, their existence can be readily documented, since authentic photos of two-headed babies are exceptionally easy to fake (all you really need are a matching pair of baby pictures, an Exacto knife, and some rubber cement). More importantly, two-headed baby stories are particularly appealing to that strange emotional mix—that unique blend of sideshow prurience and maternal compassion—that the tabloids are designed to exploit.

Though the tabloids are filled with stories celebrating the feats of "supermoms" (women whose lives are totally consecrated to the propagation and care of children), they also contain a substantial number of stories about a completely antithetical type of female: the "monster mom" or "killer granny" who engages in the most appalling kinds of child abuse. It's the rare issue of the *Weekly World News* that lacks at least one story like "CRUEL MOM KICKS TOT TO DEATH" (June 17, 1986), "COPS CHARGE MOM IN BITING DEATH OF INFANT" (May 20, 1986), or "GRANNY KILLS GIRLS TO SAVE THEM FROM SPACE ALIENS" (July 22, 1986). As Leslie Fiedler points out, one of the most important functions of the popular arts is to "express the repressed: especially the dark side of our ambivalence toward what any status quo demands we believe, and more often than not, think we do,"[36] and these stories of unnatural maternal cruelty (corresponding to folk-motifs cataloged under "Cruel Relatives" [S 0-S 99]) undoubtedly give vent to those dark, inadmissable impulses to which most full-time parents (particularly those trapped in lives of unrelieved economic oppression) are quite naturally prone.

The single most popular version of the Terrible Mother–type story is the "Sicko Swap," a variant of the folk-motif known as "Children Sold or Promised" (S 210). This is the brand of story with headlines like "MOM SWAPS INFANT SON FOR MOTORCYCLE" (*Sun*, September 23, 1986), "MOM SELLS KIDS TO BUY LOVER A CAR" (*Sun*, December 23, 1986), and "TEEN MOM SWAPS HER BABIES FOR TICKETS TO A ROCK CONCERT" (*WWN*, June 17, 1986). While these fantasies of women who dispose of unwanted children in exchange for coveted, prohibitively expensive consumer items are reported in tones of intense moral outrage, their frequent, not to say obsessive, appearance suggests that—on some deep, dark level of forbidden wish-fulfillment—they strike a highly responsive chord in the minds of millions of devoted, self-sacrificing mothers who would never (consciously) dream of such a thing.

Given the predominantly female readership of the tabloids, it's no surprise that fathers are a much less significant presence in their pages than moms. Stories about "miracle dads" do pop up from time to time. "PREGNANT MAN GIVES BIRTH" (*Sun*, July 19, 1985), "HUSBAND GIVES WIFE CAESARIAN" (*WWN*, November 19, 1985), and "MAN IS FATHER OF 1,052 KIDS" (*Sun*, December 3, 1985) are typical examples, corresponding, respectively, to the motifs of the "Pregnant Man" (T 578), "Husband as Midwife" (T 584.0.2), and "Extraordinary Number of Children" (T 586.2). For the most part, however, tabloid articles involving men tend to focus on their qualities as mates, not fathers. Almost all these pieces about wives and their "hubbies" fall into two broad, basically antithetical categories: romantic fairy tales (whose outcomes may be either tragic or triumphant) about deferred but unfading love, or, conversely, marital horror stories about spitefulness, deceit, and abuse—in short, about the condition commonly (and colorfully) referred to in the tabloids as "Wedded Blitz."

The most prevalent—and, in many ways, poignant—romantic fantasy to be found in the tabloids is the tale of the elderly lovers who, after a life-long separation, rediscover each other and achieve true happiness at last. This type of story (analogous to Motif T 96, "Lovers Reunited after Many Adventures") is a particular favorite of the *Weekly World News*, which, in virtually every issue, features at least one article like "SWEETHEARTS WED AFTER 60 YEARS" (November 19, 1986), "HIGH-SCHOOL SWEETHEARTS WHO WERE SEPA-

RATED 60 YEARS AGO MEET AGAIN" (June 10, 1986),
"TEEN ROMANCE BLOOMS AFTER 53 LONG YEARS"
(September 30, 1986), "WARTIME SWEETHEARTS RE-
UNITED" (August 5, 1986), "THEY'RE BRIDE AND
GROOM AGAIN—AFTER 50-YEAR DIVORCE!" (August
27, 1985), and "WIDOWER WOOS FIRST LOVE" (August
26, 1986). The message of hope embodied in these stories—the
assurance that, even for the rapidly aging, "there's still time,"
that it's never too late to find love[37]—is no less touching for its
essential fraudulence. Closely related to these inspirational
tales are those articles that address an apparently desperate
need to believe in love's durability—in the possibility of adoring
someone (and having that person adore you) for a lifetime. Indeed, the most striking characteristic of the tabloid romance is
that its principals are, almost without exception, senior citi-
zens: geriatric Romeos and Juliets who prefer suicide to the
prospect of life without each other ("ELDERLY COUPLE'S
LAST SUPPER—THEY GORGE ON BACON, EGGS, ICE
CREAM AND CHIPS, THEN DRINK POISON!," *WWN*,
September 2, 1986); white-haired sweethearts whose ageless passion permits them to overcome impossible odds
("COUPLE'S 48-YEAR WALK TO THE ALTAR," *WWN*, October 22, 1985); moribund mates whose devotion endures
beyond the grave ("DEATH CAN'T SEPARATE LOVING
COUPLE," *WWN*, September 3, 1985).

When it comes to wedlock, however, the tabloids have a seriously divided, not to say schizoid, attitude, and these marital
tearjerkers represent only one side of the split. The complete,
contradictory picture can be seen very clearly in the September
2, 1986, issue of the *Weekly World News*, which contains the
story of a pair of "elderly lovebirds" who commit simultaneous
suicide because they can't "bear the thought of someday being
separated by death," followed immediately by a full-page article
headlined "HUBBY DUMPS WIFE ON 25Th ANNIVER-

EXTRAORDINARY-SCENE AT A -WEDDING.

Nuptial disasters have been a popular motif in the tabloids since the nineteenth century. From the Illustrated Police News.

SARY VACATION." In the fantasyland of the tabloids, marriage, like every other aspect of day-to-day life, is a matter of the most wild extremes: of love affairs so intense that even death doesn't end them ("I'LL FIGHT TO HAVE MY DEAD HUSBAND'S BABY," *WWN*, June 24, 1986), or, alternatively, of unions so flimsy that they dissolve in a flash—often, indeed, during the wedding ceremony itself. The tabloids are rife with accounts of such nuptial fiascos: "BRIDE SAYS I DO— THEN SHOOTS HUBBY AT ALTAR" (*Sun*, December 10, 1985); "MARRIAGE FALLS APART AT WEDDING RECEPTION" (*Sun*, October 1, 1985); "WEDDING TURNS INTO BATTLE ROYAL" (*WWN*, September 9, 1986); "BRIDEGROOM FILES FOR DIVORCE 2 HOURS AFTER WEDDING" (*Sun*, December 24, 1985); "COUPLE'S MARRIAGE LASTS 2 HOURS" (*WWN*, September 17, 1985). All these articles (which fall under the general category of "Happenings at Wedding" [Motif T 150]) illustrate, once again, that tabloid stories aren't simply analogous to folklore; they *are* a form of folklore: dreamlike, or nightmarish, fantasies spun (like the magical thread in "Rumpelstiltskin") from the most homely materials.

It's interesting that the vast majority of tabloid stories dealing with marital cruelty and craziness focus, not on nasty husbands, but on the folk-figures of the "Shrewish Wife" (Motif T 251) and "Murderous Bride" (T 173). Many of these tales seem intentionally comic. Indeed, stories like "WIFE MAKES HUBBY LIVE IN DOGHOUSE" (*WWN*, September 24, 1985) and "HENPECKED HUBBY EATS HIMSELF TO DEATH TO ESCAPE NAGGING WIFE" (*WWN*, November 5, 1985) sound like scenarios dreamed up by James Thurber. Others range from the seriously unsettling ("WIFE TRIES TO KILL HUBBY WITH VAMPIRE LEECHES," *Sun*, December 10, 1985) to the actively vicious ("WIFE HIRES HOOKER TO GIVE HUBBY AIDS," *Sun*, December 10, 1985) to the downright bizarre ("ANGRY WIFE GIVES BIRTH CONTROL PILLS TO CHEATING HUBBY—HE TURNS GAY," *Sun,* October 22, 1985). Some of these folktales of wifely malice clearly reflect the standard male myths of destructive female sexuality (my personal favorite among this group is "GROOM ELECTROCUTED BY HIGH-VOLTAGE BRIDE," a full-page account in the November 5, 1985 issue of the *Sun* about a woman who "built up a large amount of static electricity" while vacuuming her wall-to-wall carpeting and then inadvertently fried her hapless hubby "during a passionate love-making session"). For the most part, however, these horror tales of "marital mayhem" seem to be straightforward revenge fantasies whose evident appeal to millions of female readers suggests something interesting about the degree of undischarged anger roiling around the ordinary American household.

If some tabloid stories offer symbolic outlets for their readers' pent-up resentments, others operate in a far more conciliatory way, encouraging women to see their mates in a favorable light. These are stories that perform what Fred E. H. Schroeder describes as one of the tabloid's major "fetish functions," which is to remind readers that "things could be worse," to admonish them to "count their blessings."[38] The most peculiar of these marital morality tales—a group of stories that constitute a separate class of tabloid folklore—deal with housewives who come to hate their hubbies, not because these men are worthless or wicked, but, on the contrary, because they are too good. The September 1, 1986, issue of the *Weekly World News,* for example, features a story headlined "TUB-OF-LARD LOSES 280 LBS AND HIS WIFE," an account of a woman who divorces her slenderized spouse because he isn't "cuddly" anymore. The message here, as in other tales of this type (e.g., "MY HUBBY'S PERFECT AND I HATE IT," *WWN,* June 10, 1986; "MOM OF SEVEN DIVORCES HUBBY BECAUSE HE'S TOO SEXY," *Sun,* January 14, 1986), seems to be that, though it's natural to daydream about the ideal male, the reality isn't all it's cracked up to be. In effect, these stories say to readers: "Sure, a slim, sexy, sensitive husband who dotes on his wife and does all of the housework sounds good in theory. But, take it from me, you're better off with what you have."

The same essential message—be grateful for what you have— is conveyed by those tabloid stories that work contemporary variations on the folk motif known as "Marriage to a Beast in Human Form" (B 651). Some of these stories transpose this traditional theme to the sci-fi age by making the "loathly bridegroom" not a disguised animal but a monster from outer space. "After being married only five months, Mrs. Joanna Feins of Gatlinburg, TN has fled from the mountaintop mobile home she shared with her husband, claiming he is a space alien," reads the lead sentence of "MY HUSBAND IS A UFO ALIEN," the headline story of the March 26, 1986 issue of the *Sun*. "'I can't believe something like this has happened to me,' declares Mrs. Feins." Much more common, however (indeed startlingly so), are stories about women who discover, to their horror, that their hubbies—men they have been married to, in some cases, for years—are actually women. "JUDGE TELLS STUNNED WIFE: YOUR HUSBAND IS A WOMAN" (*WWN*, September 17, 1985), "MY HUSBAND KEPT A SHOCKING SECRET FROM ME—HE WAS A WOMAN" (*WWN*, May 20, 1986), "WIFE DIVORCES HUBBY BECAUSE HE'S A GIRL" (*Sun*, September 3, 1985) are just a few examples of this motif. To a certain extent, these horror tales of innocent housewives who are engaged, all unknowingly, in long-term lesbian relationships are simply soft-core tabloid pornography— ways of supplying a morally upright, Middle American audience with a bit of low-level sexual titillation. Primarily, however, they represent yet another form of the "count your blessing" type story, whose underlying moral is that—whatever your mate's flaws, failings, and radical imperfections—things could be a lot worse. (At least he's a man!)

Waking up one day to discover that your bedmate is a UFO space alien or—even more appalling!—a woman is only one of many domestic nightmares that fill the pages of the *Sun* and the *Weekly World News.* Indeed, the everyday experience of the average American housewife, as it is portrayed in these papers, often seems like something straight out of a Stephen King novel. There are, in fact, notable similarities between the kind of horror-fantasy published in the tabloids and King's mega-selling brand. Like the latter, in which the most ordinary accoutrements of daily domestic life, from breakfast cereals to household pets, may suddenly turn monstrous (a device that King occasionally carries to ludicrous extremes, as in his story "The Mangler," about a demoniacally possessed laundry machine), the supermarket tabloids specialize in tales about the terrors and perils that can lurk in the most unlikely places.

To be sure, some tabloid horror stories are distinctly moralistic in tone, especially those whose apparent purpose is to gloat over the inevitably tragic consequences of unbridled adolescent behavior—for example, "PARTY PRANK FRIES TEEN" (*WWN*, February 25, 1985) or "TEEN EXPLODES AFTER DRINKING 168 CANS OF BEER" (*Sun*, November 4, 1985). Mostly, however, tabloid horror tales achieve their cheerily sensationalistic ends by depicting the grisly fates of ordinary men, women, and children who fall victim to the blood-curdling terrors of diabolical household appliances, malevolent plumbing fixtures, and fiendish convenience foods: "WOMAN DIES IN HER OWN OVEN" (*WWN*, January 21, 1986), "MAN ZAPPED BY HIS ELECTRIC EASY CHAIR" (*WWN*, October 15, 1985), "TERROR ON THE TOILET" (*WWN*, September 24, 1985), "HAIR SPRAY TURNS WOMAN IN-TO HUMAN TORCH" (*WWN*, February 4, 1986), "BOOBY

TRAPPED VACUUM CLEANER" (*WWN*, July 1, 1986),
"NOODLE STABS HOUSEWIFE" (*WWN*, December 17,
1985). Like all tabloid folklore, these homespun horror yarns
clearly illustrate the special appeal of publications like the *Sun*
and the *Weekly World News*, within whose plebeian pages miracles are commonplace while the commonplace is infused with
a childlike magic.

There are many other recurrent themes that any comprehen-
sive index of tabloid motifs would be obliged to include: the
Ghost Doc, the Psychic Tot, the Death Dream, the Super Pet,
the Celebrity Savior, the Mummy Mermaid, and more. But the
cataloging of these will have to wait until the tabloid finds its
own Stith Thompson.

It's easy enough to condescend to the tabloids. In fact, it's
hard to read through a single issue of the *Sun* or the *Weekly
World News* without breaking into superior chuckles over some
complete absurdity or other. Still, though pedagogues may well
shake their heads over these papers (whose popularity, writes
Paul Fussell, "seems to argue a total breakdown in public sec-
ondary education"),[39] folklorists ought to regard them, if not
with deep respect, then at least with a certain degree of grati-
tude. Loud, uncouth, bursting with preposterous yarns and
medieval beliefs, the supermarket tabloid offers indisputable
proof that, far from having been wiped out by modern mass culture, folk literature (like the UFO alien who assumed the shape
of Mrs. Joanna Feins' husband) has simply taken on new and
different forms.

5 The Green World

Peter Pan in America

For Chrissake, grow up.
—*J. D. Salinger,* The Catcher in the Rye

It is fashionable these days to condemn the films coming out of Hollywood as hopelessly infantile: "popcorn fantasies for kids and muppets," in the words of one disapproving critic.[1] And it is certainly true that, on any given night, moviegoers looking for a sophisticated, American-made drama—a film that renders the real world and the people in it in subtle and complex ways—are unlikely to feel overwhelmed by all the possibilities available to them. The entertainment pages of recent newspapers tend to resemble ads for a marathon, Saturday-afternoon kiddie matinee. Indeed, serious films have become such a scarce commodity on the cinematic circuit that, when a half-dozen of them opened in Manhattan movie houses in the autumn of 1986, the event was newsworthy enough to be greeted with a major piece in the *New York Times.*[2] Viewers (and reviewers) whose tastes don't run to comic-book fantasy and technological fairy tales are naturally inclined to regard today's typical Hollywood production as a sign of some deplorable, if not insidious, development and to decry the current state of American cinema (and our popular art in general) in terms that bring to mind the constant complaint of Holden Caulfield's seniors, who keep advising him to grow up.

The most far-ranging attack on the contemporary fantasy craze is an article by Kathleen Agena, "The Return of Enchantment," which appeared in the *New York Times Magazine.* Although her examples include the work of serious writers, painters, and musicians (among them Norman Mailer, Joyce Carol Oates, neoexpressionist painter Anselm Kiefer, and composer George Rochberg), the bulk of her evidence is drawn from the popular arts. Agena describes the recent craving for "fairy-tale formulas and enchantment motifs" as "scary," the "symptom of a profound crisis" in Western society. Citing a range of authorities, from Stephen Jay Gould to Harvey Cox, she argues that the phenomenal popularity of paperback bestsellers like Frank Herbert's *Dune* series and of blockbuster movies like

Star Wars and *E.T.* reflects the final collapse of the "rational theology" that has given direction and meaning to our culture since the time of the Enlightenment: the "belief that the newly arisen gods of science and technology could pave the way to Paradise."

The failure of those "gods" to make good on that promise, Agena writes, has created widespread confusion, the sense "that life and the world have lost their meaning." No longer sustained by our faith in human reason, deprived of that "shaping myth," our society is turning hungrily to "mystical symbols and motifs that hark back to notions of an enchanted universe," desperately dredging up "old gods and mysteries" in an attempt to fill up the "gaping void" created by the loss of the old "unifying vision." But that attempt, Agena concludes, is misguided at best and potentially disastrous: "The emergence of archaic, mystical motifs in the culture today represents a groping effort to find a replacement for the world view we have lost. But it does not work. What Daniel Bell has said about religion is also true of the shaping of a world view: It cannot be manufactured by political theorists or religious demagogues, but must 'grow out of the deepest need of individuals, sharing a common wakening,' and cannot be created by 'engineers of the soul.'"[3]

In seeing our recent fascination with fantasy themes as something more than a passing fad, as a trend with "larger meaning" for our lives, Agena is clearly correct. Any major pop phenomenon is a kind of cultural seismograph, revealing the large, subterranean forces that are at work beneath the surface of society (and that sometimes break through with convulsive effect). And, if anything, Agena understates the magnitude of the fantasy phenomenon, which has come to pervade every area of American popular culture. It can be seen, for example, in the immense popularity of certain toys, such as the "Smurfs," a race of roly-poly, blue-skinned gnomes that originated as a collection of small rubber figurines and have since become the center of a merchandising empire, and Mattel Company's "Masters of the Universe," a tribe of heavily armed mythological warriors led by a blond, muscle-bound character named He-Man (who looks less like a pagan demigod than an extra from a 1950s Beach Party movie). It can be found throughout the realm of rock, from the Conan-the-Barbarian album covers of the "heavy metal" group Molly Hatchet to the Night-of-the-Living-Dead imagery of Michael Jackson's phenomenally successful *Thriller* video. And it is evident in the obsessive devotion of millions of youngsters to the participatory fantasy game *Dungeons and Dragons*, along with its computerized counterparts like *Zork* and *The Sword of Kadash.*

It seems to me, however, that these and the countless other manifestations of the current fantasy-boom are not quite as scary as Agena suggests. Indeed, her response says less, in the end, about our present situation than about her own sensibility (not to mention that of the *New York Times Magazine*), which strikes me as typically Western in its one-sided devotion to rationalism and deep-seated discomfort with myth. It's easy to forget that the assumptions which underlie her argument— her belief that intuition is inherently inferior to reason; that novels containing "finely honed descriptions of daily life" are a higher form of art than those with imaginary settings; that mysticism is merely a fancy word for escapism, a woolly-headed effort "to offer a coherent world view by blurring the hard edges of reality with vague notions of oneness"—are far from axiomatic; rather, they reflect the characteristic prejudices of our culture. [4] It is, therefore, entirely possible that the mass eruption of "archaic" imagery we are witnessing right now has a very different meaning from the one set forth by Agena, whose antimythic bias leads her to see contemporary society as a kind of large-scale version of Poe's "Haunted Palace": a bastion of reason suddenly assailed by dark, irrational forces.

Agena's gloomy diagnosis of our "contemporary malaise" is

also flawed by a form of historical naiveté, a failure to see the fictions she discusses in the context of our cultural traditions. *E.T.* is a case in point. While Spielberg's film, like all pop myths, suggests a variety of meanings, it is, on one level, simply an updated version of a story that our society has needed to hear since American literature began. When Elliot and E.T. take off for the dark forest in flight from the world of grownups, what are we seeing, after all, but still another instance of the myth of the runaway male companions first identified by Leslie Fiedler—a science fiction retelling (suitable for our high-tech age and featuring an extraterrestrial buddy in place of the more traditional "alien" sidekick) of a fantasy formerly imagined in terms of cowboys and Indians, Christians and cannibals, white boys and fugitive slaves.

More seriously, there is a significant self-contradiction at the heart of Agena's argument, since, on the one hand, she clearly perceives our preoccupation with the fantastic as something that has irrupted into society with surprising force over the past few years, while, on the other, she suggests that the phenomenon has been deliberately "manufactured" by "engineers of the soul," cannily exploiting our spiritual hunger by packaging outworn symbols in flashy new forms. When Agena objects that a true myth "cannot be manufactured," she is certainly right. But her implication that "the return of enchantment" is somehow prefabricated flies in the face of her own evidence, which makes it clear that what we are witnessing at present is a collective phenomenon with deeply unconscious sources. There's no doubt that large sums of money are being generated by this trend and that many people are cashing in on it. This is, after all, America—"the culture of commodities," in Christopher Lasch's phrase[5]—and even the gods (when they choose to manifest themselves here) are quickly transformed into consumer goods. To a nonbeliever, an Elvis Presley Limited Edition Commemorative Liquor Decanter may be just another piece of all-American kitsch. But that doesn't diminish its iconic power one bit for the thousands of worshippers who convert their family playrooms into shrines to "The King" or make yearly pilgrimages to Graceland.

What I'm suggesting, in short, is that, far from having a purely negative significance, the reverence for child's fantasy that has gripped America in recent years can be seen as a positive force: the sign, not of the complete absence of a functioning myth, but, on the contrary, of the appearance of a genuine and vital mythic archetype, carrying a weight of symbolic meaning into the cultural mainstream. Interestingly, one of the experts Agena cites in her article, James Hillman, makes this very point (which Agena, however, chooses not to pursue), attributing our current situation to the culture-wide activation or "evocation" of the "child archetype."[6] Hillman is America's preeminent Jungian theorist, and to understand just what the "child archetype" is and why it has taken such a firm hold on our collective imagination, it will help to look briefly at Jung's own ideas about the nature and function of archetypal myth.

I should say at this point that, in spite of my serious reservations about many of Jung's theories and the highly reductive uses to which they're often put by his followers, I find much of value in his work. Partly because he is such a ponderous writer (especially when compared to Freud) and partly because he set himself the task of talking scientifically about intuited concepts that are essentially inarticulable (a mythic symbol being, by definition, the incarnation of a mystery, "a token of the ineffable," in J. J. Bachofen's phrase),[7] Jung's ideas are easy to misunderstand, distort, and even make fun of (so that, for example, the "collective psyche"—by which he means, simply, that fundamental level of the mind which is the source of our typically human perceptions and responses, our ways of behaving in and relating to the world—is commonly misrepresented as a "racial memory," as though all of us, somewhere deep inside our heads, carry around shared recollections of living in caves and hunting mastodons for dinner). And, of course, his ideas are not susceptible of "proof." Finally, I suppose, believing in the validity of what Jung has to say is largely a matter of faith—but then again, so is a belief in Freud. (I think it was a recent biographer of Cotton Mather who pointed out that, during the seventeenth century, ascribing aberrant behavior to the workings of Satan was no more or less superstitious than attributing it in our own day to that unseen, demonic force we call the unconscious.)

To me, certain of Jung's insights are very persuasive, and one of his most interesting and, I think, useful ideas is that mythic symbols, capable of exerting a "strange, compelling power,"[8] have a tendency to arise in response to any serious imbalance in the conscious life of a single person or an entire society. The corollary of this notion is that compulsive behavior, again in either an individual or a group, can only be completely understood when we see it as a symbol and not merely (in the way of traditional psychoanalysis) as a neurotic symptom.

Jungian analyst Edward C. Whitmont gives the example of a middle-aged patient—a strong-willed, "overly rational" businessman with an inability to "express feeling" or establish close personal relationships—who found himself possessed by a severe foot fetish, "unable to function sexually with any woman except through first licking or kissing her feet."[9] Read symbolically, this neurosis reveals itself as a compensatory urge to pay homage to "the Goddess," to recognize and venerate that "feminine" realm of "feeling and instinctual involvement" that had been pathologically neglected by the patient. Thus, Whitmont concludes, this person's illness can actually be interpreted as a (desperate) push toward psychic equilibrium: an effort to force him into an awareness of the dangerous "onesidedness" of his orientation and to "connect him with a dimension of his being from which his life had become separated at the price of sterility."[10]

Jung's theory of compensation can also account for mass compulsions. It seems likely to me, for example, that the exercise mania, the new religion of fitness, which has swept our country over the past few years is a cultural reaction to the ascendancy of the computer: that America's sudden collective need to worship the body is a kind of unconscious protest against (and corrective to) our growing dependence on the electronic brain. (If, as J. David Bolter suggests, every age has its defining piece of technology, ours is not only the computer but its complement, the Nautilus machine.)[11]

The phenomenon Jung describes—the way a compensating symbol can suddenly break into a suffering or uncentered society and exert a compelling influence on the lives of large numbers of people—is strikingly portrayed in Steven Spielberg's science-fiction blockbuster, *Close Encounters of the Third Kind.* The movie focuses on a character named Roy Neary (Richard Dreyfuss), a modern-day, working-class Everyman inhabiting a dreary midwestern wasteland that is the visible projection of the state of Neary's (and, by extension, the contemporary American) soul. Neary's life is utterly sterile, mundane to the point of deadliness: an endless and empty round of nine-to-five drudgery, cheerless consumerism, and stifling domesticity in a tacky suburban development. Clearly he (along with the other people who share his experience) is in desperate need of something more in his life—and when that something suddenly appears, it is (as we should expect, following Jung's theory of compensation) the exact opposite of the mundane, a symbol of precisely what's missing from Neary's soulless, workaday existence.

The religious overtones of Spielberg's movie (which were apparently even more pronounced in Paul Schrader's original screenplay)[12] have been noted by various critics. Neary undergoes the sci-fi version of a mystical experience: what thrusts itself into his world is a technological incarnation of the divine, a celestial city of light inhabited by angelic creatures. This visitation forces Neary into an awareness of a higher dimension of being. He becomes a kind of Holy Madman—a blue-collar visionary, journeying to the mountaintop to gaze upon his gods and offer himself into their service. *Close Encounters,* then, shows how a symbol can seize us, individually or communally, compelling us to pay attention to an area of our lives that we have neglected, lost touch with, or undervalued at the expense of our emotional (or spiritual) health. On one level, Spielberg's film is a story about what Jung calls "modern man in search of a soul" and its central symbolism is (in a general way) religious.

On another level, however, *Close Encounters* is about the importance of staying in touch with a childlike part of ourselves that we denigrate or forget at our own risk. Ultimately, the power that Neary is brought into contact with and that redeems his life from stagnation is an emanation, not from heaven or outer space, but from the depths of the psyche, symbolizing this inner, indestructible (though often neglected) child principle. The immediate effect of Neary's "close encounter" with this power is to turn him back into a kid: his face becomes flushed with an innocent joy and he transforms his dreary living room into a giant sandbox, where he spends his time sculpting a colossal mud castle.

The human specimens brought aboard the alien craft—the young World War II pilots, for example, whose planes are discovered during the opening moments of the film—are, if not rejuvenated, then preserved in a state of perpetual youth; "they return from space," as Morris Dickstein notes, "without having aged."[13] And the occupants of the UFO "mother ship" are, appropriately enough, a flock of radiant star-children (played, for the most part, by real kids): cuddly descendants of the dreamy-eyed space-embryo envisioned at the end of Kubrick's *2001* and prototypes of Spielberg's fullest realization of the "child archetype," E.T. In short, *Close Encounters of the Third Kind* can be seen as a fable about the phenomenon Agena describes: the invasion of America by the forces of enchantment—the powerful spell that has been cast over our culture by the myth of eternal childhood.

At the same time, the movie makes it clear that Agena is wrong to see this phenomenon as specific to the past few years, since, in spite of having been released in 1977, *Close Encounters* is a work which, as Dickstein also points out, is markedly a distinctly "60s sensibility."[14] To understand the current significance of the child archetype for our society, then, we should start by considering how and why it arose in the sixties, specifically in the counterculture. Actually, it's probably less accurate to say that the counterculture gave rise to this archetypal symbol than the reverse—i.e., that the symbol created the counterculture—since the youth movement of the sixties was, I believe, a dramatic illustration of the kind of mass possession Jung talks about: the way important but disregarded values can penetrate into a society in the form of powerful, mythic images which come to dominate the imaginations and determine the behavior of entire groups. In the sixties counterculture, we see just such a phenomenon: a generation of people possessed by and living out a myth—in this case, the one Hillman refers to as the child archetype and which is known in Jungian psychology as the *puer aeternus*, the Eternal (or Immortal) Child.

Jungians see the mythic image of the *puer aeternus*—the "divine youth" of Classical and Oriental religions, embodied in gods like Adonis and Tammuz—as a metaphor for an indestructibly childlike part of the human personality. The term itself, according to Marie-Louise von Franz (who, along with Hillman, has done the most writing on the subject), derives from Ovid's *Metamorphoses*, where it is "applied to the child-god in the Eleusinian mysteries," Iacchus.[15] Frequently, *puer* figures are vegetation spirits, young male deities who die and are reborn in the spring. Sometimes, like Narcissus and Hyacinthus, they are resurrected in the form of flowers; they are, as Hillman points out, "flower people," flower children.[16] Other well-known examples of the *puer* archetype include Attis, Dionysus, Hippolytus, Hermes, and Pan.

As a psychological symbol, the *puer* stands for a combination of character traits associated with the fantasy of perpetual youth, eternal childhood. The *puer* personality is dominated by a rejection of adulthood, a longing to drop out of time. Refusing to enter the "father's" world of power, control, and acquisition, a world which is constantly threatening to ensnare him, to bring him "down to earth,"[17] the *puer* is subject to particular impulses and desires: acute feelings of restlessness and a fear of being bound (to a lifetime job or a single lover); a sense of becoming diminished or devitalized by such mundane ties; fantasies of running away or taking flight (an aspect of *puer* psychology symbolized by the myths of Icarus and Bellerophon); and a vague but powerful sense of "homesickness," a yearning to return to the "Mother," to a lost paradise of enveloping love and "privileged irresponsibility."[18]

This enchanted, "maternal" realm—this place of perennial summer outside the vicissitudes of time—is typically associated with (Mother) Nature: Northrop Frye, finding examples of it in the magical forests of Shakespeare's comedies, calls it "the green world."[19] Perhaps for this reason, the *puer* personality often has an affinity for flowers and plants, a desire to "get back in touch with nature" (the *puer* figures of folklore and myth are often the son-lovers or brother-husbands of Earth Mother Goddesses: e.g., Attis-Cybele, Tammuz-Ishtar, Osiris-Isis). In keeping with the *puer*'s preadolescent character, there is, at times, something distinctly androgynous about him: a "hermaphroditic quality where masculine and feminine are so perfectly joined that nothing else is needed."[20] Finally, the *puer* is distinguished by a tendency to prize "childlike" qualities (innocence, spontaneity, gentleness, imagination) over those "grown-up" attributes (shrewdness, determination, tough-mindedness, discipline) which society most values as the requisites of worldly success.[21]

All these characteristics can be clearly seen in J. M. Barrie's Peter Pan, probably the most famous pop avatar of the *puer* archetype—the child-principle incarnate. Peter's ability to fly is a symbol of both his refusal to be bound to the mundane world and his flight from adulthood. The sworn enemy of the Father, whose darkest aspects (greed, rapacity, aggression) are embodied in the villainous Captain Hook, Peter will not accept the laws of time (the play is subtitled "The Boy Who Would Not Grow Up").[22] He fled his home as an infant, he tells Wendy, because he heard his "father and mother talking about what I was to be when I became a man" (p. 32); and when Mrs. Darling later offers to adopt him, he refuses, saying, "No one is going to catch me, lady, and make me a man" (p. 157); that is, turn him into a replica of her husband, that sober-minded paterfamilias and "breadwinner" (p. 11) enslaved to his office and the stock exchange.

An emissary from the Never-Land, a green, fairy realm accessible only to those who have not yet made the fall into maturity, Peter occasionally touches down in the real world but recoils from anything that threatens to tie him to it, including a relationship with a possible mate: when Wendy, early in the play, "leaps out of bed to put her arms around him," Peter, the stage directions inform us, "draws back; he does not know why, but he knows he must draw back" (p. 29). "You mustn't touch me," he tells Wendy, and when she asks why, he only repeats, "No one must ever touch me" (p. 29). Like the young vegetation gods of ancient mythology, Peter is a nature spirit as well as the personification of eternal youth: he is dressed, "in so far as he is dressed at all," in "autumn leaves and cobwebs" (p. 27) and makes his home in a hollow tree. Moreover, again like such son-lovers as Tammuz and Adonis, he is in thrall to the Mother. At the heart of Barrie's play, as Howard Kissel points out, is a powerful obsession: a yearning after the lost mother "so strong that in the first production there was a scene in which Peter puts an ad in the London paper asking for 'Beautiful Mothers' to adopt the

Lost Boys."[23] Kissel also draws attention to Peter's androgynous nature, his "sexual ambiguity," noting that, since the first performance of *Peter Pan* in 1904, "a woman has always played the title character."[24]

It's no accident that "I Won't Grow Up," Peter Pan's theme song introduced in the 1954 Broadway-musical version starring Mary Martin, and "My Generation," the Who's hard-rock, sixties anthem with its defiant cry "Hope I die before I get old," express essentially the same sentiment. For in every respect, from the fashions it wore to the kind of art it produced, from its politics to its sexual styles, the sixties generation behaved in absolute accordance with the archetypal pattern of the *puer aeternus*, with what one pop-psych writer (playing on the title of Laurence Peter's bestselling book) has called the "Peter Pan Principle."[25]

The counterculture had all the hallmarks of a true religious movement: a multitude of people suddenly gripped by a resurgent myth, by the archaic symbol of the Flower Child. Perceiving its enemies as real-life Captain Hooks (buccaneering politicians and child-killers), the counterculture recommended "dropping out" (of society, of history) and retreating to the Green World, to that Never-Land of nature, love, and magic that John Lennon called "Strawberry Fields."[26] In opposition to the values of the Father (to "daddy politics"[27] and the Protestant work ethic), it exalted the virtues, pleasures, and playthings of childhood. In place of weapons, toys (kaleidoscopes, prisms, frisbees, windchimes). In preference to High Literature, fairy tales (like Tolkien's *The Lord of the Rings*) and comic books (like *Zap* or *The Fabulous Furry Freak Brothers*). Instead of gray-flannel suits, kiddie clothing and Halloween-party costumes (in the sixties, writes Alison Lurie, "an observer on the main street of any large city in . . . America might see persons dressed up as babies, grandmothers, cowboys, pirates, gypsies, Indians, soldiers, Christian hermits, Oriental sages, Robin Hood, and Little Bo Peep").[28]

The traditional American virtues of enterprise and industry were scorned: the go-getter was replaced by the Holy Innocent, a type of character (otherworldly, childlike, ill-equipped to deal with the "real world") endlessly celebrated in that era's story and song. (Vonnegut's Billy Pilgrim, the protagonist of *Slaughterhouse-Five, or, The Children's Crusade,* is a prime example, as is Benjamin Braddock, the hero of that cinematic sixties fairy tale *The Graduate.*) In rock, the Holy Innocent myth can be found throughout the music of the Beatles (the preeminent minstrels of the *puer* state of mind), though it is, perhaps, most strikingly embodied in their song "The Fool on the Hill."

In other ways, too, the counterculture conformed precisely to the archetypal pattern of the Eternal Child: in its glorification of Mother Nature; its celebration of the "rambling" way of life (of picking up and "movin' along the highway," particularly when a personal relationship threatens to become too emotionally demanding);[29] its androgynous (or "unisex," in the terminology of the time) styles; and even in its devotion to drugs (the most effective way of flying off to the Never-Land, in the absence of Tinker Bell's fairy dust). What I'm suggesting, in short, is that the youth movement of the sixties did not grow simply (or even primarily) out of political or utopian goals; rather, it was the manifestation of a myth: a "primordial image" come to life and clothed in bell-bottom jeans, beads, and fringed buckskin jackets.

It is possible, of course, to see the hippies as simply a bunch of spoiled kids, bent on prolonging their adolescence and indulging in various "regressive" pleasures: polymorphous perverse (instead of procreative) sex; getting high instead of getting down to business. But it's important to recognize that the use of the word regressive to describe childlike interests says less, in the end, about those interests than about the dominant attitudes of our rigidly rationalistic culture, which perceives human development from infancy to old age as a strictly linear progression (akin to climbing the corporate ladder) and views the persistence of "the child" in the adult as a serious character flaw, a failure to advance according to schedule or, even worse, as a step in the wrong direction. As a mythological symbol, however, the child represents, not something negative, not a vestige of values we ought to outgrow, but, on the contrary, crucially important qualities too easily forgotten in our intense focus on the world of getting and spending. When the child myth begins to assert itself, to raise itself into the consciousness of an entire society (as was the case, I believe, in the sixties), we would do well to consider it in light of Jung's theory: as a symbol "whose purpose is to compensate or correct, in a meaningful manner, the . . . one-sidedness and extravagances of the conscious mind."[30]

If we ask what condition brought the *puer aeternus* myth to the surface of our culture in the sixties, what dangerously "unbalanced" situation it arose in response to, the answer, I believe, is clearly the Vietnam War: our immersion in a particularly ugly and (self-)destructive military venture. In symbolic terms, the child is the opposite of war and violence—a fact recognized in the frequent use of the child image in the propaganda of the peace movement, such as posters showing young Vietnamese victims of napalm attacks and the slogan (reproduced on everything from stationery to drinking glasses), "War isn't healthy for children and other living things."

While the latter smacks somewhat of Hallmark-card sentimentality, the symbolic opposition between the child-image and killing has, in fact, a firm biological basis. In a fascinating essay on the "progressive juvenilization" of Mickey Mouse, his evolution from a rambunctious "ratty character" to a "cute and inoffensive" one, Stephen Jay Gould cites Konrad Lorenz, who "argues that . . . features of juvenility trigger 'innate releasing mechanisms' for affection and nurturing in adult humans. When we see a living creature with babyish features, we feel an automatic surge of disarming tenderness."[31] Lorenz's strictly biological theory goes a long way toward supporting Jung's supposedly "mystical" one, suggesting that the child-symbol is a genuine archetype, that is, a universal image that elicits (in Gould's words) "powerful emotional responses" in human beings;[32] and that among the various emotions and "meanings" evoked by the child-symbol, one of the most important is non-aggression—the child functions as a "psychological corrector,"[33] an instinctive (Jung would say archetypal) response to violent tendencies.

The appearance of the child as a healing symbol in the midst of bloodshed and horror can be seen clearly in that quintessentially sixties movie *M*A*S*H*, where the only sane response to the madness of war is a retreat to the Dennis-the-Menace pranksterism of its heroes, Hawkeye and Trapper John, or to the holy innocence of Radar O'Reilly, who sleeps in his army cot at night cradling a teddy bear. The redemptive power of the child in a war-ravaged world is also a central theme in some of J. D. Salinger's early stories. "For Esmé—With Love and Squalor," in which a single, loving gesture from the thirteen-year-old title character saves the battle-shocked narrator from insanity and despair, is the most famous of these, though the theme is also present in three of Salinger's uncollected stories from the forties, "The Last Day of the Last Furlough," "A Boy in France," and "The Stranger,"[34] all of which focus on a young soldier named Babe Gladwaller and his ten-year-old sister, Mattie, who embodies that painfully vulnerable innocence and purity that Salinger venerates throughout his work.

I bring up Salinger because any discussion of the Eternal Child myth in contemporary America has to acknowledge his profound impact on the baby-boom generation that brought that myth to life in the sixties. In regard to the counterculture, Holden Caulfield—who, like his mythic brethren, undergoes a very real death and rebirth in the course of his fictional development (after being killed, or at least reported missing in action, in a story set during WW II, he is resuscitated, rejuvenated, and returned to civilian life in *The Catcher in the Rye*)—is as seminal a figure as any of the Beats, in spite of his distinctly non-bohemian way of life. He is a preppy Peter Pan whose attitudes and perceptions—his contempt for grownups and reverence for childhood, his desire to drop out and escape to the Green World (he longs to "get the hell out of" New York and run off to the woods of Vermont)—had a determining influence on the values of the generation that came of age in the sixties and regarded Salinger's book as one of its earliest bibles. As much as anyone, then, Holden Caulfield helped give birth to the sixties, but, by a curious and bitter irony, he also helped bring them to a close. In a very striking way, Salinger's book brackets the era, for if we can point to a single symbolic event that decisively marks the end of the "Aquarian Age," it would surely be the murder of John Lennon by Mark David Chapman, a young man who identified closely with Holden and who, after gunning down the rock idol, calmly sat down to read *The Catcher in the Rye* while waiting for the police to arrive.

Obviously, however, the sixties Peter Pan myth has not become extinct in America. If anything (as the evidence amassed by Kathleen Agena makes quite clear) its hold over our collective imagination is stronger and more extensive than ever. Partly this is because some of the most powerful forces in the popular arts are themselves the products of that era—people like George Lucas, Steven Spielberg, Stephen King, and John Landis—and their work inevitably reflects a countercultural sensibility. You have only to glance at the way George Lucas habitually dresses on a movie set—in blue jeans, workshirt, and running shoes—as compared to the fashions affected by, say, Cecil B. DeMille to get a vivid sense of how thoroughly the sixties style has permeated Hollywood. As any number of critics have noted, Lucas' *Star Wars* "saga" is entirely informed by sixties attitudes: the exaltation of the child, the interest in some kind of quasi-Oriental religion ("The Force"), the sentimental view of nature's superiority over technology, as represented by the ultimate triumph of those furry, forest creatures, the Ewoks, over the death-machines of the evil Empire. (That *Star Wars* itself represents a substantial triumph of state-of-the-art technology is the kind of paradox that has never troubled anyone before; after all, if it weren't for ultramodern recording facilities and vinyl-processing plants, John Denver wouldn't exist, either.)

Stephen King's novels are full of the same kind of sixties child-reverence, though, because his métier is horror, his vision is considerably darker. Virtually all of his books—*Carrie, Salem's Lot, The Shining, Firestarter, Cujo, Pet Sematary*—focus on children threatened or destroyed by the grownup world, doomed to suffer for the crimes and craziness of adults (often their parents). Spielberg's movies tend to alternate between Lucas' brand of action-adventure and the creepshow entertainments of King. What's special about Spielberg is the powerful sense of "childlike wonder" that infuses his films; the vision that runs throughout most of his work is of the normal world suddenly transformed by an irruption of the fantastic in either a malevolent (*Duel, Jaws, Poltergeist*) or benign (*Close Encounters, E.T.*) form. To go to a Lucas or Spielberg movie—to the latest installment of *Star Wars* or the adventures of Indiana Jones—has become a kind of American seasonal ritual, a celebration of the return of summer, a two-hour trip to the Green World of childhood (a fantasy made explicit in 1985's Spielberg-produced, summer blockbuster *Back to the Future*).

That the Peter Pan myth has come to dominate our communal fantasy life as never before is apparent in the remarkable popularity of Spielberg's *E.T.*, the top-grossing film in Hollywood history. In trying to account for its amazing success, critics have compared its title character to a wide range of figures, from the enchanted toad of the Grimm Brothers' stories to

Christand.[35] It is evident from the sheer number of people who have been deeply affected by the film that it must work on various levels; no single meaning can account for its phenomenal and far-reaching appeal. It has the suggestive (if ultimately elusive) quality of a genuine myth.

For very young children, *E.T.* is clearly a wish-fulfillment fantasy about an imaginary playmate—or, more precisely, about a favorite *plaything* come to life. As the film's various visual references to characters like Yoda and Bobba Fett suggest, E.T. is a preadolescent boy's dream-come-true: a living, breathing *Star Wars* action figure. There are other, somewhat more complex kinds of wish-fulfillment that Spielberg's film offers young children. Lévi-Strauss' notion that myths bring together irreconcilable polarities—resolve "the fundamental and discomforting contradictions of experience"[36]—is certainly borne out by E.T., who mediates a host of oppositions: human/animal, earth/heaven, male/female, head/heart, nature/technology, and—very strikingly—child/adult. For if (as the film's numerous allusions to Barrie's play make clear) E.T. is an extraterrestrial Peter Pan, he also serves as an embodiment of ageless wisdom, a mythological Wise Old Man and replacement for Elliot's absent father. Clearly, this is a potent fantasy for the millions of American children who, like Elliot, have suffered through their parents' divorce. (It's interesting to see how common this theme has become in the movies. A partial list of contemporary films containing characters who are searching for surrogate, or actual, fathers, includes, besides *E.T., Star Trek II, Annie, Return of the Jedi, Rocky III, An Officer and a Gentleman, The Karate Kid,* and *Top Gun.*)

Perhaps the most important way *E.T.* functions for children, however (in terms of its unconscious "message"), is as a kind of kindergarten version of "The Secret Sharer." When we first meet Elliot, the young hero of the movie, he is insecure, isolated, inept: a "blossoming neurotic" (in the words of William

Kotzwinkle's best-selling novelization) who is regarded by his teenage brother's friends as a thoroughgoing "twerp."[37] Like the narrator of Conrad's famous story, however, he discovers—and keeps hidden in his bedroom—a mysterious alter ego. E.T. (whose name, as several critics have pointed out, is a truncated form of the hero's) is also isolated, graceless, and not much to look at (the physical resemblance between Elliot and E.T. is made explicit in Kotzwinkle's book, where the extraterrestrial is described as having "bulbous eyes . . . the kind you might find on a giant frog," while the boy wears "thick glasses that make him feel like a frog").[38]

But E.T. is also the possessor of tremendous powers and, through him, Elliot comes to discover his own inner strengths. By the end of the film he has been transformed from a twerp into a competent and self-assured young man—a junior John Wayne who exudes confidence (one charming scene shows E.T. sitting at home watching John Ford's *The Quiet Man* on TV while Elliot, who has established a close psychic bond with the extraterrestrial, sweeps a pretty young classmate off her feet with the Duke's inimitable style) and commands the respect of the older boys who formerly made fun of him.

The three-hundred-or-so million dollars that *E.T.* earned, however, did not all come out of the pockets of preadolescents. On the contrary, the audiences that waited in lines to see the film and left the theaters in tears were composed in large part of an older generation—the generation that Spielberg himself is a member of, which is to say the so-called baby-boomers. To them (us, I should say), E.T. conveys a very different set of messages.

One of these, I believe, has to do with E.T.'s looks. As Spielberg's sometime-collaborator, Lawrence Kasdan, makes clear in *The Big Chill* (one of whose principal characters is a former sixties radical who has grown rich from a chain of athletic-footwear shops called "Running Dogs"), the Woodstock Generation has grown up to become the Jogging Generation, and there is something deeply appealing for this group, I believe, about a hero who is so blithely unconcerned about his body. E.T. is an intergalactic Garfield the Cat: roly-poly, intensely homely, addicted to junk food (in the novel he is an avid consumer of M&M's, Oreo cookies, and ice cream). That characters like these (the Muppets' Miss Piggy and the chocoholic hippos of Sandra Boynton are other examples) have achieved enormous popularity during the very height of the fitness craze in this country suggests that they serve a therapeutic function for millions of people. They are the tricksters-gods of the shape-up age, thumbing their noses at the health-food gurus and the disciples of Jane Fonda. In their cheerful defiance of the current standards of beauty and fitness, they provide some healthy release for whatever secret resentments the rest of us may feel toward the prevailing tyrannies of diet and exercise.

More significantly, Spielberg's movie is a totally contemporary version of the age-old myth of the Eternal Child. All the characteristics of the classical *puer aeternus* figures are combined in E.T.: He has the ability to fly and a fear of being earthbound (the *puer*, says Hillman, feels "weak on earth because he is not at home on earth").[39] He experiences intense homesickness (the symptom of a longing for the lost Mother, who is embodied here in the science fiction form of E.T.'s departed mother ship). He is clearly a nature spirit, a creature who emerges from the Green World that exists just outside Elliot's enclosed suburban community. His sexuality is highly ambiguous (Carlo Rambaldi, the special effects wizard who constructed E.T., apparently conceived of the alien as a member of an androgynous species).[40] And he undergoes a dramatic death and resurrection. Moreover, ancient as he is (centuries-old, according to Kotzwinkle's novel), E.T. is still very much a cuddly, starry-eyed space child who waddles and speaks like a toddler, has a powerful sweet tooth, and does his best to stay away from grownups.

The *puer* figure most consistently invoked in *E.T.* is, of course, Peter Pan, who seems central to Spielberg's personal mythology. Indeed, Spielberg has been quoted as saying, "I think I'm Peter Pan, I really do,"[41] and visual allusions to Barrie's fairy tale appear not only throughout *E.T.*[42] but also in *Close Encounters of the Third Kind* (the "Red Whoosh"—the cute little UFO that skitters after the rest of the fleet—is strikingly reminiscent of Walt Disney's Tinkerbell) and Spielberg's contribution to the *Twilight Zone* movie, "Kick the Can" (which, unlike the original TV version, ends with the image of a swashbuckling youngster hovering at an open window, precisely like Peter Pan at Wendy's bedroom, and then taking off into the night). Moreover, for a few years, reports persisted that Spielberg was planning to direct a musical remake of Barrie's play starring Michael Jackson.

In the end, what gives Spielberg's movie its special resonance for the (aging) children of the Vietnam era is the way it embodies sixties values and ideals in a form that speaks directly to the eighties—the way it gives new life to old myths by casting them in specifically contemporary (i.e., computer-age) terms. To me, *E.T.* is less a leprechaun, Christ figure, or enchanted frog than a high-tech hippie, a flower-child from the most technologically advanced civilization in the cosmos, who, along with his comrades, has come to earth on a conservationist mission in an atomic-powered greenhouse (a conceit that apparently derives from Douglas Trumbull's countercultural space-epic *Silent Running*, about an idealistic scientist who fights to preserve earth's last remaining flora in a kind of orbiting botanical garden).

It's no accident that the plum of writing the *E.T.* novelization went to William Kotzwinkle, a sharp-eyed chronicler of the counterculture whose hilarious novel *The Fan Man* is the definitive portrait of a zonked-out hippie acid-head. As Kotzwinkle's numerous references to elves and orcs suggest, E.T. is a direct descendant of Tolkien's fantasy creatures. But he is also—as his ability to whip together an interplanetary radio transmitter from a bunch of household odds and ends makes clear—a mechanical genius. He is, in short, a hobbit with computer-age skills, a perfect amalgam of sixties nature-child and eighties whiz-kid. In this sense, *E.T.* is the cinematic equivalent of the "US Festival" organized a few years ago by Apple cofounder Stephen Wozniak which was itself an effort to reconcile the values of Woodstock with those of Silicon Valley. *E.T.* reassures us that it is possible to be a member of a high-tech civilization without being turned into a machine. In short, one of the primary meanings of Spielberg's film is not simply how important it is for adults to stay in touch with the childlike parts of their personalities but how vital it is for our entire culture to bring the sixties ethos of peace, love, and reverence for nature into the computer age if we are to escape its potentially dehumanizing effects.

E.T. is only one sign that the Peter Pan myth which first manifested itself in (or through) the counterculture has begun to assert itself with renewed force in recent years. In the fall of 1983, *Esquire* magazine ran a cover story called "The Peter Pan Principle" (subtitled "When Men Won't Grow Up"); almost simultaneously, a pop-psych book called *The Peter Pan Syndrome: Why American Men Won't Grow Up* hit the nonfiction bestseller lists. Meanwhile, *Greystoke,* Hugh Hudson's lavish retelling of the Tarzan legend which became one of the big box office hits of 1984, brought the *puer aeternus* myth to the screen. Its hero is a noble (and perfectly innocent) savage who dashes back to his primordial Green World after a brief sojourn in a society absolutely inimical to the Child (the film is full of images of dead baby apes that have been slaughtered by Great White Hunters or dissected by scientists, and when the movie's most sympathetic elderly character, Ralph Richardson in the role of the hero's grandfather, attempts to recapture his childhood by sliding down a few stairs on a silver tray, he is instantly killed).

The most striking sign of the *puer*'s presence in American culture during the 1980s, however, has been the phenomenal success of Michael Jackson's *Thriller* album, which sold an astounding thirty-five million copies within a year of its release in 1982. The parallels between Jackson and Peter Pan have been noted by a number of critics, including *Time* magazine's Jay Cocks, whose cover story on the singer points out various links between Jackson and earlier embodiments of the *puer* archetype: The Beatles (Jackson, who is "smitten with . . . their mystique," has collaborated on several occasions with Paul McCartney and befriended Sean Ono Lennon); E.T. (Jackson narrates the children's record based on the film and appears on the album cover with his arm around the alien); and Disney (Jackson is an avid collector of old Disney cartoons and, according to Cocks, "takes trips to Disney park as to a shrine"). Cocks speculates, in fact, that the single white glove Jackson affects— so similar to the ones worn by Disney characters—is a conscious tribute to the animated creatures the singer loves.[43]

But if Jackson is like any Disney character at all it is not Mickey Mouse or Goofy. Rather, with his doelike eyes and delicate features, he seems related to Bambi (a resemblance that has apparently occurred to Steven Spielberg, who is quoted in Cocks' article as saying, "Michael can be hurt very easily. He's sort of like a fawn in a burning forest"). Indeed, this association suggests the reasons for the sudden resurgence of the *puer* myth in America, for *Bambi* is Disney's heartfelt (if typically sentimental) protest against mankind's penchant for destruction. And it is no accident that Jackson achieved his extraordinary popularity at the precise moment when the fear of nuclear annihilation gripped our civilization with renewed force—that the two most talked-about phenomena of the fall of 1983 were *Thriller* and "The Day After," the controversial TV movie about World War III.

The Eternal Child myth first took possession of the counter-culture, I believe, as a result of the Vietnam War, and if it now holds sway over our culture at large, that may be because the peril we face at present is even graver. In my view, the "return of enchantment" to America is the sign of a spontaneous and essentially healthy impulse, an attempt (by that instinctive part of ourselves that prefers life over death) to pull us away from a potentially catastrophic course by exalting values antithetical to war; in short, not a neurotic retreat to the past but an eminently sane bid for a future.

Epilogue

The "Jason" Legend:
The Symbiosis of
Popular Art and Folklore

As I was finishing the final draft of this study, a news story appeared in my local paper which so perfectly illustrates one of the main points I've been making that something like synchronicity seems to be at work. Academic "purists" will undoubtedly go on regarding the American entertainment industry as a vast, soulless power that is relentlessly trampling authentic folklore underfoot—the cultural equivalent of one of H. G. Wells' Martian war machines, busily obliterating every piece of human handiwork in its path. It seems to me, however, that the incident in question not only offers incontrovertible proof of the reciprocal relationship between the popular arts and folklore but also sheds considerable light on the ways in which the two serve to feed off of, and nourish, each other.

As I mentioned in my first chapter, the folkloric sources of various contemporary "slasher" films—those blood-drenched dismemberment fantasies so dear to the hearts of the drive-in crowd—have been amply documented by a number of folklore scholars, most notably Larry Danielson. [1] For various reasons, most of them having to do with the standard sexual fears and confusions that attend adolescence, teenagers dote on low-grade gore flicks. [2] It seems only natural, therefore, for exploitation filmmakers to lift their material from those gruesome little spook stories that have provided sure-fire frissons in dormitories and frat houses for decades. As Danielson demonstrates, films like *Halloween, When a Stranger Calls,* and *Silent Night, Evil Night* are simply feature-length elaborations of these widely known legends, all of which focus on one or another avatar of the contemporary teenager's favorite bogeyman, the implacable psycho-killer, whose single-minded purpose is to prey on unwary teenage couples, too busily engaged in the back seat of the Chevy to hear the buzz of the approaching chainsaw or the scrape of the sharpened steel hook on the handle of the car door.

A particularly instructive instance of this process—i.e., the transformation of a local horror-legend into a hardcore splatter film—can be seen in the case of Wisconsin sex-butcher Ed Gein, whose connection to Tobe Hooper's *The Texas Chain Saw Massacre* was discussed in an earlier chapter. Within weeks of the discovery of Gein's "house of horrors" (as *Life* described it)—his white-clapboard abattoir, decorated with the body parts of dismembered middle-aged women—his crimes had already entered into regional folklore in the form of sick jokes, ghoulish songs, and spook stories, a phenomenon which drew the fascinated attention of various psychiatrists, who saw it as striking example of the way a traumatized community copes with an unimaginably awful event. The May 1959 issue of the *Bulletin of the Menninger Clinic,* for example, contains an article by Wisconsin psychiatrist George W. Arndt which describes the craze for Gein-inspired gallows humor that was sweeping the state. Much of this humor took the form of ghoulish riddles called "Gein-ers" (e.g., Why was the heat always turned on in Ed Gein's house? So the furniture wouldn't get goose bumps. What did they find in Ed Gein's cookie jar? Lady Fingers). In a later, expanded version of his essay, Arndt also reproduced a parodical version of Clement Moore's famous poem which demonstrates quite clearly Gein's metamorphosis, in the popular imagination, from a psychiatric case-study into a genuinely mythic monster, a back-country bogeyman with distinctly diabolical powers:

'Twas the night before Christmas, when all through the shed,
All creatures were stirring, even Old Ed.

The bodies were hung from the rafters above,
While Eddie was searching for another new love. . . .

He sprang to his truck, to the graveyard he flew,
The hours were short and much work must he do.

He looked for the grave where the fattest one laid.
And started in digging with shovel and spade. . . .

He took out a crowbar and pried open the box,
He was not only clever, but sly as a fox.

As he picked up the body and cut off her head,
He could tell by the smell that the old girl was dead. . . .

He let out a yell as he drove out of sight.
If I don't get caught, I'll be back tomorrow night![3]

Particularly in the minds of younger Wisconsinites, Gein quickly assumed supernatural shape. Indeed, for a whole generation of Wisconsin children, the night-specter that lurked in their closets and haunted their dreams took the form of "Crazy Ed." In a fascinating piece on Gein, Wisconsin writer David Schreiner describes the impact of Gein's crimes on the collective psyche of his peers: the epidemic of nightmares that plagued their sleep; the dread that descended even on the older children as nighttime drew near; the hysteria that could be set off by the invocation of Gein's name (Schreiner relates the case of a girl who "ran screaming from her house and out into the street, where she was struck . . . by a truck, after her older brother threatened to 'Gein her'").[4] Ultimately, this oral folklore was transmuted into film, completing Gein's evolution from a singularly deranged psychopath to a figure in local legendry to a character who has become part of our shared cultural mythology. Whereas *Psycho* derived from newspaper accounts of Gein's atrocities (Robert Bloch, the author of the original novel, was living in Milwaukee when Gein's crimes were uncovered),[5] Tobe Hooper's notorious fright film grew out of the bedtime stories he heard in his childhood when visiting midwestern relatives would spook him with tales of the Wisconsin ghoul.[6] This folkloric background undoubtedly accounts in part for the dark, fairy tale flavor of *The Texas Chain Saw Massacre*—its close resemblance to some of the grimmest of the Grimm Brothers' stories.

Though Hooper's film remains the undisputed masterpiece of the genre, the *Citizen Kane* of dismemberment movies, the biggest money-maker of the bunch has been Sean Cunningham's *Friday the 13th*, which to date has spawned five sequels plus a syndicated TV series. The original film—the opening chapter in a cinematic splatter-epic that promises (or threatens) to continue forever—deals with an isolated summer camp whose oversexed, adolescent staff members are dispatched in a variety of colorful ways by an implacable homicidal maniac. The surprise ending reveals the psycho-killer to be none other than Betsy Palmer (of TV's "I've Got a Secret" fame), playing the vengeful mom of a grotesquely deformed child named Jason Vorhees, a former camper who, we are told, had drowned years before while his sex-crazed caretakers were busily disporting themselves on the nearest available bunk bed. Though *Friday the 13th* has obvious parallels to that archetypal horror tale "Hansel and Gretel," it is more directly derived from the kind of adolescent apocrypha—the legends about local maniacs who prey on unwary vacationers—that are a staple of sleepaway camp folklore.

The phenomenal box-office success of Cunningham's film produced the inevitable "Part II," in which Jason is resurrected in order to carry on his mother's life work of butchering sexually active teenagers. Decked out in his trademark hockey mask and possessed of a natural genius for contriving creative forms of slaughter, Jason has pursued his one-man crusade against adolescent promiscuity since 1981 and shows no sign of slowing down. Indeed, in 1984 the producers decided to end the series with *Friday the 13th, Part IV: The Final Chapter.* The movie, however, made so much money that Jason was brought back to life (again!) in the following year's *Friday the 13th, Part V: A New Beginning,* a title which clearly deserves a place of honor in the exploitation-movie Hall of Fame.

Most remarkable of all, Jason, the hulking, hockey-masked star of the series, has become a genuine cult figure among gore-film devotees, who array themselves in "Jason Lives" T-shirts, adorn their bedroom walls with full-color posters of their sub-human hero, and read of his further blood-drenched exploits in paperback "novelizations." The high esteem in which Jason is held by horror fans is wittily conveyed in an article by self-professed "gorehound" Charles Balun. Published in *Fangoria,* a slick newsstand magazine devoted to "horror in entertainment," Balun's piece is an amusing analysis of "Jasonmania" that is part parody of highbrow horror-film criticism, part heartfelt tribute to "the Sultan of Slaughter":

> It's difficult to focus precisely on the enormous appeal that a brain-damaged, misshapen, machete-wielding Momma's boy can have over a receptive public. But, hell, who knows for sure about anything these days? Jason could be a modern embodiment of some primeval, vengeful spirit that

haunts the wicked or he could be simply an agent of catharsis, acting out our deepest, most deranged and violent desires. Through his bloodletting, we are purged and relieved of the homicidal tension building within us. Really—who hasn't thought of corkscrewing his boss/teacher/boyfriend/girlfriend's hand to a cutting board, burying a meat cleaver in their forehead, or nailgunning their whimpering butt right to the wall?

Jason as myth hmm . . . let's think a moment here. This guy couldn't possibly survive all the machete mayhem, hatchet-whacking, and other attacks upon his person without *some* sort of supernatural powers. There's much, much more to this lump-headed, gap-toothed King of Carnage than one would ever guess. [7]

"Jason indeed lives," Balun concludes—and the rumor I referred to at the start of this postscript certainly seems to bear him out. That rumor first arose in the fall of 1986 and spread rapidly throughout the suburban county I reside in, culminating in what newspapers described as "a bizarre Halloween panic." Here is the story as it appeared on page one of my local paper, the Westchester *Reporter Dispatch*, October 31, 1986:

SLAYING REVIVES RUMORS OF "CHILD-KILLER"

Cops Flooded with Calls from Worried Parents

Police in three counties said Thursday that their emergency phone lines were clogged with calls from parents whose children have been hearing rumors that a man dressed as a horror movie character is stalking the area.

The rumors, which began last month in the Stormville area of Dutchess County, had died down until the murder Saturday of Marjorie Myers-Lodes, police said.

Mrs. Myers-Lodes, 25, was stabbed about 40 times in her home in Shenorock section of Somers.

On Tuesday, Terrance Murnane, 24, of Tighe Road in Somers, was arrested and charged with second-degree murder.

State police in Stormville last month investigated reports that a prankster wearing a hockey mask—like the "Jason" character in the "Friday the 13th" film series—terrorized children walking home from school. Wednesday, after a month without leads or further incidents, the case was closed.

But Sgt. Raymond Kennedy of the Stormville barracks said the rumors—and worried calls from parents—resumed after Mrs. Myers-Lodes was killed.

Saying the murder has left a "lingering nervousness" with many Westchester parents, Sgt. David Spahl of the state police barracks in Somers warned, "Everyone's still upset about what happened. But at this point, nothing like what these kids have heard has been borne out by our investigations."

The movie "Friday the 13th" was broadcast Thursday over a local television station.

What makes this urban (or, more precisely, suburban) belief tale so significant is not that it springs from a film. As scholars like Donald Allport Bird, Ronald L. Baker, and Jan Harold Brunvand have pointed out, many modern legends—from the "Paul McCartney Death Rumor" to "Michael Jackson's Telephone Number"—have been bred by the mass media.[8] The story of the Westchester child-killer is remarkable for a different reason: it is a striking, perhaps singular, instance of a contemporary legend generated by a film which is itself the product of a narrative folk-tradition. Behind the creation of this regional myth, in short, is a cyclical process in which a piece of oral folklore (the widespread tale of the sleepaway-camp psycho-killer) was transmuted into a movie (*Friday the 13th*) which, in turn, gave birth to a new variant of the legend (the "Jason" rumor). Thus, this "bizarre Halloween panic" reveals the working of a flourishing symbiosis between folklore and popular art. And, perhaps more importantly, it offers convincing proof that, even in this age of high-tech entertainment, the impulse to create and consume folklore is as powerful as ever—indeed, as lively and indestructible as the "King of Carnage" himself.

Notes

1. The Bosom Serpent

1. King, *Night Shift*, p. xx.
2. Harris, "Brand-Name Horror," p. 43.
3. Fiedler, "Giving the Devil His Due," p. 199.
4. Dickstein, "Peter Panavision," p. 21.
5. Panofsky, "Style and Medium," p. 33.
6. Fiedler, "Giving the Devil His Due," p. 197.
7. Ibid., p. 200.
8. Stephen King, who describes it as his favorite statement of the pop writer's overriding commitment to sheer "story value," quotes Burroughs' line in his foreword to *Night Shift*, p. xxi.
9. Leach, "Folklore in American Regional Literature," p. 395.
10. Bausinger, "Folklore Research," p. 127.
11. Dégh, "The 'Belief Legend' in Modern Society," p. 59. In a later essay, Dégh is even more emphatic, asserting that "it is not enough to acknowledge that mass media has a 'role' in modern legend-transmission. It is closer to the truth to state that the mass media are *part* of folklore." See Dégh and Vázsonyi, "The Dialectics of the Legend," p. 37.
12. Baker, "The Influence of Mass Culture," pp. 367–376.
13. In his essay "A Theory for Folklore in Mass Media," Bird discusses the "Paul McCartney Death Rumor" as a "multimedia event . . . fusing with folklore processes." See p. 290.
14. Baker, "The Influence of Mass Culture," p. 368. Cf. Brunvand's observation that "today's legends are also disseminated by the mass media" in *The Vanishing Hitchhiker*, p. 3. As early as 1943, a contributor to the *Journal of American Folklore* noted that contemporary folklore "may be viewed as functioning through literature and drama—both of which are recognizable today by their mechanical accompaniments, printed matter and radio." See Smith, "Musings on Folklore, 1943," p. 72.
15. Russell, "Folktales and Science Fiction," pp. 3–30.

16. A variety of folklore analyzed with characteristic lucidity and insight by Dundes. See "The Dead Baby Cycle," pp. 145–157.

17. Brunvand, *The Vanishing Hitchhiker*, p. 5.

18. Ibid., p. 6.

19. White, "A Persistent Paradox," p. 122.

20. See, for example, Motifs X 1721 ("Lies about Surgical Operations"), X 1786 ("Lies about Healing"), and E 321 ("Dead Husband's Friendly Return") in Baughman, *Type and Motif-Index*.

21. Ibid., Motif G 297.

22. Danielson, "Folklore and Film," pp. 209–219. For recorded texts of these urban legends, see ibid., p. 218, n. 15 and Brunvand, *The Vanishing Hitchhiker*, pp. 47–73.

23. Danielson, "Folklore and Film," pp. 214, 217.

24. Brunvand, *The Vanishing Hitchhiker*, pp. 112f.

25. Ibid., pp. 90f.

26. Maslin, "Hippie Nostalgia," p. 16.

27. Brunvand, *The Vanishing Hitchhiker*, p. 65.

28. Ibid., pp. 24f.

29. Ibid., pp. 47–73.

30. Dundes, "On the Psychology of Legend," p. 30.

31. H. R. Ellis Davidson, "Folklore and Literature," *Folklore* 86 (1975): 87.

32. Shortly after this chapter was completed and submitted in essay form to the *Georgia Review* (where it appeared in the spring 1985 issue), Jan Harold Brunvand came out with his second study of urban legends, *The Choking Doberman*, which mentions both "Egotism" and *Alien* in a section on "Bosom Serpent" legends. To keep the scholarly record straight, then: although Professor Brunvand and I seem to have been meditating on this subject at around the same time, his published comments on the connection between Hawthorne's story and Ridley Scott's movie preceded mine by a year or so.

33. Hawthorne, "Egotism, or, the Bosom Serpent," in *The Celestial Railroad and Other Stories*, p. 171. All further references to this story appear in the text.

34. See Arner, "Of Snakes and Those Who Swallow Them," pp. 336–346.

35. Ibid., p. 337.

36. Partridge, "Notes on English Folklore," p. 313.

37. Arner, "Of Snakes and Those Who Swallow Them," p. 346.

38. Ibid.

2. The Bloody Chamber

1. Prawer, *Caligari's Children*, pp. 6ff.
2. *The Complete Grimm's Fairy Tales*, pp. 534–535.
3. Campbell, "Folkloristic Commentary," p. 860.
4. Emily Dickinson, "There's a certain Slant of light" (J. 258).
5. King, *Danse Macabre*. King is not only the preeminent contemporary practitioner of terror-fiction, "the master of modern horror," as the advertising blurbs say; he is also one of its shrewdest theoreticians, though *Danse Macabre*, for all its very real intelligence, is a seriously off-putting work. What makes it finally so annoying is partly King's prolixity but even more so his tone. In all of his public statements, King comes across as an engagingly unassuming individual, no different (give or take several million dollars) from the ordinary devotee of E.C. comics, *Famous Monsters of Filmland*, and the movies of George Romero. But while his "plain-fiction-for-plain-folks" persona works to his advantage as a novelist, it results in an unpleasantly— indeed obnoxiously—hypocritical brand of criticism in which he resolves the conflict between his anti-elitist sentiments and the inherently elitist nature of his undertaking by ridiculing his intellectual sources, in fact by ridiculing intellectuals and academics in general. Throughout the book, King strains to ingratiate himself with his hypothetical audience by sneering at anything that the average subscriber to *Spiderman* comics might consider a load of bull (as King would put it)—Freud, for example. At the same time, his insights clearly come directly out of his own academic training. The results are often unattractive—there's a pervasive sense that King is currying favor with the philistines—and at other times fairly amusing, as when he interprets the Jekyll and Hyde story as a "pagan conflict between man's Apollonian potential and Dionysian desires" and then defines the Dionysian as the "get-down-and-boogie side of human nature" (p. 83).
6. Ibid., pp. 132–133, 176ff.
7. Ibid., p. 133.
8. Howard Nemerov, "Lore," in *Mirrors & Windows: Poems*, p. 74.
9. Freud, *Totem and Taboo*, p. 58.
10. Ibid., pp. 58–59.
11. The connection between this advertisement and the ending of *Carrie* has been noted by *New York Times* film critic Vincent Canby, who calls the ad for *The Evil Dead* a "direct lift from the climactic mo-

ment" of De Palma's film. See the *New York Times*, April 24, 1983, section 2, p. 17.

12. Campbell, "Folkloristic Commentary," pp. 861–862.

13. Bettelheim, *The Uses of Enchantment*, p. 101.

14. John McCarty, *Splatter Movies*, p. 1.

15. King, *Danse Macabre*, p. 132.

16. Brighton, "Saturn in Retrograde," p. 73.

17. Ibid., p. 76.

18. Fiedler, *What Was Literature?*, pp. 41–42.

19. Hoberman and Rosenbaum, *Midnight Movies*, p. 289.

20. Hartland, "The Forbidden Chamber," p. 289.

21. *The Complete Grimm's Fairy Tales*, p. 217.

22. Hartland, "The Forbidden Chamber," p. 209. Cf. the Grimm Brothers' story "The Robber Bridegroom," discussed elsewhere in this chapter.

23. Ibid., p. 193.

24. Ibid., p. 210.

25. Ibid., p. 207.

26. *The Complete Grimm's Fairy Tales*, p. 217.

27. Hartland, "The Forbidden Chamber," p. 202.

28. Bettelheim, *The Uses of Enchantment*, p. 302.

29. Von Franz, *An Introduction to the Interpretation of Fairy Tales*, chapter 7, p. 43.

30. Hartland, "The Forbidden Chamber," p. 193.

31. See, for example, Captain James Cook's account of a Tahitian sacrifice, "the earliest scientifically recorded anthropological document" of this taboo. Reprinted in Campbell, *The Mythic Image*, pp. 430ff.

32. Melville, *Typee*, p. 238.

33. Barham, *The Ingoldsby Legends*, p. 205.

34. Campbell, "Folkloristic Commentary," pp. 862, 860.

3. The Giant's Toy

1. Biskind, *Seeing Is Believing*, p. 4.

2. Ibid., pp. 141, 144.

3. King, *Danse Macabre*, p. 133.

4. Ibid., p. 290.

5. Lyons, "King of High-School Horror," p. 76.

6. Opie, *The Classic Fairy Tales*, p. 12.

7. Thompson, *The Folktale*, p. 106.

8. Thompson, *Motif-Index of Folk-Literature*.

9. Bettelheim, *The Uses of Enchantment*, pp. 66ff.

10. Opie, *The Classic Fairy Tales*, p. 15.

11. Christopher Lehmann-Haupt, review of *The Talisman* by Stephen King and Peter Straub, *New York Times*, November 8, 1984, section C, p. 27.

12. King, *Danse Macabre*, p. 318.

13. Campbell, *The Masks of God*, pp. 21–29.

14. Opie, *The Classic Fairy Tales*, p. 31.

15. Eliade, *Myths, Dreams, and Mysteries*, p. 36, and *Myth and Reality*, p. 192.

16. Eliade, *Myths, Dreams, and Mysteries*, pp. 36–37.

17. Ibid., pp. 34–35, and *Rites and Symbols of Initiation*, p. 127.

18. Eliade, *Myths, Dreams, and Mysteries*, pp. 36, 34.

19. Ibid.

20. The phrases come from Penn Warren's famous and widely anthologized story "Blackberry Winter," which stands as one of the most lyrical evocations of this "primordial, paradisiacal" realm in our literature.

21. Opie, *The Classic Fairy Tales*, p. 33.

22. Ibid., p. 34. Subsequent references in my text are to this edition.

23. Fetuses, of course, exert a powerful, primitive fascination, especially on children (as the sideshow popularity of preserved human embryos—"pickled punks" in the parlance of the carnival—attests). And, indeed, tales of the Thumbling hero may ultimately derive, I believe, from this archaic response, that is, represent a way of managing or defusing the anxieties provoked in us by the sheer uncanniness of the fetus.

24. *The Complete Grimm's Fairy Tales*, p. 193.

25. Opie, *The Classic Fairy Tales*, p. 31.

26. Thompson, *The Folktale*, p. 86.

27. Opie, *The Classic Fairy Tales*, pp. 32–33.

28. In Stephen King's *Danse Macabre*, Matheson describes the circumstances surrounding his conception and creation of *The Shrinking Man* (the original title under which the book was published in

1956) but makes no mention at all of Tom Thumb. See King, *Danse Macabre*, pp. 319ff.

29. Matheson, *The Incredible Shrinking Man*, p. 132. Subsequent references in my text are to this edition.

30. Fiedler, *Freaks*, p. 64.

31. Opie, *The Classic Fairy Tales*, p. 34.

32. Crawford, "Georges Méliès," pp. 27–30, 56.

33. Darnton, *The Great Cat Massacre*, pp. 13, 15, 16.

34. *The Complete Grimm's Fairy Tales*, pp. 212ff.

35. Opie, *The Classic Fairy Tales*, p. 34.

36. Prawer, *Caligari's Children*, p. 60.

37. King, *Danse Macabre*, pp. 325, 326.

38. Biskind, *Seeing Is Believing*, p. 264. For a recent, highly readable look at the tensions and anxieties behind "the canonized version of fifties family life," see Eisler, *Private Lives*, esp. chapter 10. According to Eisler, "Men, especially journalists most likely to write of such matters (and even likelier to prefer a few drinks after work to going home and putting the kiddies in bed), lost no time in equating the new ethos [of togetherness] with the emasculation of the American male" (p. 221).

39. Friedan, *The Feminine Mystique*, p. 204.

40. The last of these fantasies—that of being turned into a human doll or puppet by an awesomely oversized female—corresponds to the folktale known as "The Giant's Toy" (Type 701 in the Thompson index). Literary examples of this fantasy can be found in works ranging from *The History of Tom Thumbe* to *Gulliver's Travels*.

41. *Man's Life*, November 8, 1959, p. 12f. and *Man's Action*, November 1, 1959, pp. 4f.

42. Steranko, *History of Comics—Volume One*, p. 41.

43. McLuhan, *The Mechanical Bride*, pp. 68–69. The view of married life embodied in *Blondie* is, of course, relatively benign. Far more disturbing are the visions contained in the famous line of horror comics—*Weird Fantasy, The Vault of Horror, The Haunt of Fear, Tales from the Crypt*, etc.—produced in the 1950s by E.C. These publications, which aficionados regard as the greatest comic books of all time and which have exerted a major influence on contemporary creators of horror, including Stephen King, George Romero, and Tobe Hooper (director of *The Texas Chain Saw Massacre* and *Poltergeist*), are pervaded by a powerful fear of women. As King writes in *Danse Macabre*,

"In almost all the weird comics of the '50s, the women are seen as slightly overripe, enticingly fleshy and sexual, but ultimately evil: castrating, murdering bitches who, like the trapdoor spider, feel an almost instinctual need to follow intercourse with cannibalism" (p. 35).

Interestingly, two stories from the E.C. line—published several years before the appearance of Matheson's book—bear striking parallels to *The Incredible Shrinking Man*. In "Shrinking from Abuse" (*Weird Fantasy* 11 [January/February 1952]), a miserable old mad scientist, who treats his timid, cringing wife with constant and undisguised contempt, accidentally injects himself with a shrinking formula and somehow ends up swimming around in his wife's cup of tea, whereupon she promptly gulps him down. A far more interesting and unsettling story appears in *Weird Fantasy* 16 (November/December 1950). Called "Second Childhood," it deals with another elderly mad scientist who falls in love with his nubile assistant and invents a rejuvenating potion to make himself more attractive to her. After they are married, however, he keeps getting younger and younger, until, at the very end of the story, he is literally and completely infantilized. The last panel of the comic shows the poor wife cradling her baby-husband in her arms, feeding him a bottle. Like *The Incredible Shrinking Man*, this story is a funny-horrific parable of neurotic regression, reflecting the characteristically fifties condition Wyndham Lewis calls "mothering-wedlock."

44. Biskind, *Seeing Is Believing*, pp. 250ff.

45. These films are, in essence, futuristic variants of the folk motif known as the "Journey to the Land of Women" (F112). According to schlock film specialists Harry and Michael Medved, who relate the postwar popularity of "prehistoric women" movies to the sexual and domestic fantasies of the "returning vets," more than two hundred of these films have been churned out by Hollywood since "the trend began in the early 1950s." See *Son of Golden Turkey Awards*, pp. 153f.

46. Although there is some ambiguity in the film about the nature of Scott's military service, the original novel indicates that Scott was "with the Infantry in Germany" (p. 75).

47. Thurber's cartoon is reprinted in *Alarms & Diversions*, p. 308.

48. A *Mad* magazine parody of Carl Sandburg's "Chicago"—quoted by Peter O. Muller in his book *Contemporary Suburban America*, p. 2—nicely sums up the financial stresses inherent in the suburban dream:

Show me a suburb with mortgage payments so high that
men worry themselves into heart attacks at forty,
Debt-ridden,
Overdrawn,
Embezzling,
Financing, de-faulting, re-financing.

It's not hard to see how the effort to support such a crushing burden
could make any struggling suburban breadwinner (someone like Scott
Carey, for instance) feel very small indeed.

49. King, *Danse Macabre*, p. 329.

50. For example, see Weigle, *Spiders & Spinsters*.

51. Like virtually all giant spider movies, the film version of *The Incredible Shrinking Man* features a tarantula, a far more photogenic (if less symbolically suggestive) creature than the black widow.

52. Hartland, *English Fairy and Other Folk Tales*, pp. 281–282. Cf. Steel, *English Fairy Tales*, pp. 213–214.

4. The Killer Granny

1. Fiedler, *What Was Literature?*, pp. 136–137.

2. Ibid., p. 21.

3. DeVries, *'Orrible Murder*, introduction.

4. Ibid., p. 138.

5. Fiedler, *What Was Literature?*, p. 145.

6. Collected in Panofsky, "Style and Medium," in *Awake in the Dark*, p. 33.

7. Ibid. In examining the "folk-art character of the primitive film," Panofsky mentions the memorable cinematic moment when "the head of Mary Queen of Scots actually comes off"—a reference to the Edison Company's 1893 kinetoscope short, *The Execution of Mary Queen of Scots*, a thirty-second movie which (true to its title) consists of nothing more than a shot of a costumed actress stepping up to the block and being decapitated. It's worth pointing out that this film— which is, in effect, an *Illustrated Police News* engraving come to life— marks the earliest use of a movie special effect (stop-motion photography, which allowed a dummy to be substituted for the actress before the blade came down). The progression from the Victorian tabloid to the Edison filmstrip to a movie like *Friday the 13th* suggests that the

history of popular entertainment consists, to a large extent, of the ongoing efforts of its creators to find new and increasingly realistic ways of showing people being cut to pieces and killed.

8. DeVries, *'Orrible Murder*, p. 7. This supposedly true story, which involves a mouse that darted into a man's mouth and remained alive inside his body, gnawing at his chest until "the unfortunate fellow died . . . in the most horrible agony," has connections to both the "bosom serpent" motif and the contemporary urban legend of the "Kentucky Fried Rat." See Brunvand, *The Vanishing Hitchhiker*, pp. 81f.

9. DeVries, *'Orrible Murder*, p. 111.

10. Brunvand, *The Choking Doberman*, pp. 3ff.

11. Ibid., p. 48.

12. Motif E 422.1.11.3.

13. S. T. Moore, "Those Terrible Tabloids," quoted in Simon Michael Bessie, *Jazz Journalism*, p. 19.

14. Dégh and Vázsonyi, "The Dialectics of the Legend," p. 37.

15. Ibid.

16. MacDougall, *Superstition and the Press*.

17. McCluhan, *The Mechanical Bride*, p. 3.

18. Ibid.

19. Bessie, *Jazz Journalism*, p. 17.

20. MacDougall, *Superstition and the Press*, pp. 266–267.

21. Dégh and Vázsonyi, "The Dialectics of the Legend," p. 34.

22. The term *foaf* was coined by English folklorist Rodney Dale in his book *The Tumor in the Whale* and adopted by Jan Harold Brunvand in *The Choking Doberman*, pp. 50f.

23. Dickson and Goulden, *There Are Alligators in Our Sewers*, p. xvi.

24. Malcolm W. Browne, "Fossils Point to Giant Ape's Violent End," *New York Times*, November 11, 1986, section C, p. 1.

25. Schroeder, "*National Enquirer* Is National Fetish!," pp. 168–181.

26. Fussell, *Class*, p. 142.

27. Prose, *Bigfoot Dreams*, pp. 192–193.

28. Fussell, *Class*, p. 142.

29. Schroeder, "*National Enquirer* Is National Fetish!," p. 168.

30. Prose, *Bigfoot Dreams*, p. 30. Cf. Kurt Vonnegut's observation regarding "*The American Investigator*" (i.e., the *National Enquirer*) in his novel *God Bless You, Mr. Rosewater:* "The issues with which the paper dealt were eternal" (p. 107).

31. Schroeder, *"National Enquirer* Is National Fetish!," pp. 175–176.

32. *Weekly World News,* September 30, 1986 and the *Sun,* October 28, 1985. Bizarrely enough, I did encounter a parallel to the first of these stories in, of all places, the December 26, 1986 issue of the *New York Times* (section B, p. 3). The story, headlined "MAN IS WARDED OFF WITH FUDGE SUNDAE," concerned a middle-aged woman who beat off an attacker with a dish of ice cream—further proof (as though any were needed) that modern American life can sometimes match the weirdest imaginings of a tabloid writer.

33. Prose, *Bigfoot Dreams,* p. 3.

34. See, for example, Bernheimer, *Wild Men in the Middle Ages;* Dudley and Novak, *The Wild Man Within;* Husband, *The Wild Man;* and Fiedler, *Freaks,* pp. 154f.

35. "Style and Medium in the Motion Pictures," in *Awake in the Dark,* p. 33. This *Weekly World News* story also has parallels to Motif T 475.2.1, "Intercourse with Sleeping Girl."

36. Fiedler, *What Was Literature?,* p. 41.

37. See Prose, *Bigfoot Dreams,* p. 192.

38. Schroeder, *"National Enquirer* Is National Fetish!," p. 175.

39. Fussell, *Class,* p. 142.

5. The Green World

1. Dickstein, "Peter Panavision," p. 21.

2. Janet Maslin, "The Fall's Best Movies Rate a G, for Grown-Ups," *New York Times,* November 21, 1986, section C, p. 1.

3. Agena, "The Return of Enchantment," p. 80.

4. For an incisive discussion (and lively critique) of America's deep-seated antagonism to "the non-intellective powers of the personality," see Roszak, *The Making of a Counter Culture,* esp. pp. 53f. and chapter 7.

5. Lasch, *The Culture of Narcissism,* p. 22.

6. Agena, "The Return of Enchantment," p. 76.

7. Jacobi, *Complex/Archetype/Symbol,* p. 78.

8. See Alan MacGlashan, "Daily Paper Pantheon," *The Lancet,* January 31, 1953, p. 239.

9. Whitmont, *The Symbolic Quest,* p. 20.

10. Ibid., p. 23.

11. See Bolter, *Turing's Man.*

12. See, for example, Crawley, *The Steven Spielberg Story,* pp. 59f., and Short, *The Gospel from Outer Space,* pp. 29f.

13. Dickstein, "Peter Panavision," p. 21.

14. Ibid.

15. Von Franz, *Puer Aeternus,* p. 1.

16. "Senex and Puer: An Aspect of the Historical and Psychological Present," in *Eranos-Jahrbuch 1967,* p. 330.

17. Hillman, "Pothos: The Nostalgia of the *Puer Aeternus,*" in *Loose Ends: Primary Papers in Archetypal Psychology,* pp. 50–52.

18. Brown, *Life against Death,* p. 24.

19. Frye, "The Argument of Comedy," p. 66.

20. Hillman, "*Senex* and *Puer,* p. 328.

21. The title character of Willa Cather's "Paul's Case" is perhaps the most complete representation of the *puer aeternus* archetype in American fiction. Hillman finds literary examples in "St. Exupery, in Shelley, Rimbaud, in Rousseau; Shakespeare's Hotspur is an example; Herman Melville has at least five such beautiful sailor-wanderers." See Hillman, "Pothos," p. 57.

22. Barrie, *Peter Pan.* Page numbers given in my text refer to this edition.

23. Kissel, "Peter Pan," pp. 22–23.

24. Ibid.

25. Hellerstein, "The Peter Pan Principle," pp. 64ff.

26. Another common name for it at the time was Middle Earth. I remember a mock travel poster—a popular wall decoration in sixties dorms and "crash pads"—showing a psychedelic landscape and reading "Come to Middle Earth." Cf. Peter Beagle's introduction to Tolkien's *Lord of the Rings:* "In terms of passwords, the Sixties were the time when the word *progress* lost its ancient holiness and escape stopped being obscene. [Middle Earth offers] a green alternative to each day's madness in a poisoned world." (Quoted by Updike in *Hugging the Shore,* p. 284.)

27. Roszak, *The Making of a Counter Culture,* p. 4.

28. Lurie, *The Language of Clothes,* pp. 82–83.

29. The quoted lyric comes from Carole King's song "So Far Away" from her *Tapestry* album. This sixties "highway fantasy" is perhaps best exemplified by the movie *Easy Rider* and some of the early lyrics of Bob Dylan, whose second album is called *The Freewheelin' Bob Dylan* (a later release is titled *Highway 61 Revisited*). Dylan's song

"Don't Think Twice It's All Right"—in which the singer tells his lover, "When the rooster crows at the break of dawn / Look out your window and I'll be gone"—is one of the classic pop formulations of this fantasy.

30. Hillman, "Abandoning the Child," in *Loose Ends*, p. 12.

31. Gould, "Mickey Mouse Meets Konrad Lorenz," p. 34.

32. Ibid., p. 36.

33. Hillman, "Abandoning the Child," p. 12.

34. "The Last Day of the Last Furlough," *Saturday Evening Post*, July 15, 1944, pp. 26–27, 61–62, 64; "A Boy in France," *Saturday Evening Post*, March 31, 1945, pp. 21, 92; "The Stranger," *Colliers*, December 1, 1945, pp. 18, 77.

35. See, for example, Nelson, "The Alien Already Here," p. 1, and Short, *The Gospel from Outer Space*, pp. 61ff.

36. For an excellent application of Lévi-Strauss' theory to a popular work, see Kelly, "More than a Woman," pp. 235–247.

37. Kotzwinkle, *E.T. the Extraterrestrial*, p. 38.

38. Ibid., p. 39.

39. Hillman, "*Senex* and *Puer*," p. 326.

40. See Crawley, *The Steven Spielberg Story*, p. 140.

41. Ibid., p. 9.

42. See ibid., pp. 115f. and Short, *The Gospel from Outer Space*, pp. 62f.

43. Cocks, "Why He's a Thriller," pp. 54–60.

Epilogue

1. Danielson, "Folklore and Film," pp. 209–219.

2. For a perceptive discussion of the connections between teenage sexuality and the contemporary horror movie, see Twitchell, *Dreadful Pleasures*, esp. pp. 65ff.

3. George W. Arndt, "Gein Humor," repr. in Gollmar, *Edward Gein*, pp. 206–207.

4. Schreiner, "Ed Gein and the Left Hand of God," p. 29.

5. Ibid., p. 28.

6. See Carson, "'Saw' Thru," pp. 10–11.

7. Balun, "Jason: The Sultan of Slaughter," pp. 14–16, 67.

8. See Bird, "A Theory for Folklore in Mass Media," pp. 285–305; Baker, "The Influence of Mass Culture," pp. 367–376; and Brunvand, *The Mexican Pet*, pp. 181ff.

Works Consulted

Agena, Kathleen. "The Return of Enchantment." *New York Times Magazine*, November 27, 1983, pp. 68–80.

Aitken, Barbara. "Scraps of English Folklore, VII." *Folk-Lore* 37 (1926): 78–80.

Aldrich, Charles Robert. *The Primitive Mind and Modern Civilization.* New York: AMS Press, 1969.

Arner, Robert D. "Of Snakes and Those Who Swallow Them: Some Folk Analogues for Hawthorne's 'Egotism; or, the Bosom Serpent.'" *Southern Folklore Quarterly* 35 (1971): 336–346.

Atkins, Thomas R. *Graphic Violence on the Screen.* New York: Monarch Press, 1975.

Atteberry, Brian. *The Fantasy Tradition in American Literature: From Irving to Le Guin.* Bloomington: Indiana University Press, 1980.

Baker, Donald. *Functions of the Folk and Fairy Tales.* Washington, D.C.: Association for Childhood Education International, 1981.

Baker, Ronald L. *Hoosier Folk Legends.* Bloomington: Indiana University Press, 1982.

———. "The Influence of Mass Culture on Modern Legends." *Southern Folklore Quarterly* 40 (1976): 367–376.

Balun, Charles. "Jason: The Sultan of Slaughter." *Fangoria* 62 (1978): 14–16, 67.

Barham, Richard Harris. *The Ingoldsby Legends.* 1860; repr. London: Everyman Library, 1960.

Barnes, Daniel R. "Some Functional Horror Stories on the Kansas University Campus." *Southern Folklore Quarterly* 30 (1966): 309–310.

Barrie, J. M. *Peter Pan.* New York: Scribner's, 1928.

Baughman, Ernest W. "The Cadaver Arm." *Hoosier Folklore Bulletin* 4 (1945): 30–32.

———. *Type and Motif-Index of the Folktales of England and North America.* Indiana University Folklore Series no. 20. The Hague: Mouton, 1966.

Bausinger, Hermann. "Folklore Research at the University of Tübingen." *Journal of the Folklore Institute* 5 (1968): 124–133.

Berne, Eric. "The Mythology of the Dark and Fair: Psychiatric Use of Folklore." *Journal of American Folklore* 72 (1959): 1–13.

Bernheimer, Richard. *Wild Men in the Middle Ages: A Study in Art, Sentiment, and Demonology.* Cambridge, Mass.: Harvard University Press, 1952.

Bessie, Simon Michael. *Jazz Journalism: The Story of the Tabloid Newspapers.* New York: E. P. Dutton, 1938.

Bettelheim, Bruno. "The Art of Moving Pictures." *Harper's,* October 1981, pp. 80–83.

———. *The Uses of Enchantment: The Meaning and Importance of Fairy Tales.* New York: Alfred A. Knopf, 1976.

Bird, Donald Allport. "A Theory for Folklore in Mass Media." *Southern Folklore Quarterly* 40 (1976): 285–305.

Biskind, Peter. *Seeing Is Believing: How Hollywood Taught Us to Stop Worrying and Love the Fifties.* New York: Pantheon Books, 1983.

Bolter, J. David. *Turing's Man: Western Culture in the Computer Age.* Chapel Hill: University of North Carolina Press, 1984.

Bonaparte, Marie. "The Myth of the Corpse in the Car." *American Imago* 2 (1941): 105–126.

Briggs, Katherine. *An Encyclopedia of Fairies.* New York: Pantheon Books, 1967.

———. *The Fairies in English Tradition and Literature.* Chicago: University of Chicago Press, 1967.

Brighton, Lew. "Saturn in Retrograde, or the Texas Jump Cut." In *Graphic Violence on the Screen,* Thomas R. Atkins, ed. New York: Monarch Press, 1975.

Britton, Andrew, et al. *American Nightmare: Essays on the Horror Film.* Toronto: Festival of Festivals, 1979.

Brown, Norman O. *Life against Death.* Middletown, Conn.: Wesleyan University Press, 1959.

Browne, Ray B., ed. *Objects of Special Devotion: Fetishes and Fetishism in Popular Culture.* Bowling Green, Ohio: Bowling Green University Popular Press, 1982.

Brunvand, Jan Harold. *The Choking Doberman and Other "New" Urban Legends.* New York: Norton, 1984.

———. *The Mexican Pet: More "New" Urban Legends and Some Old Favorites.* New York: Norton, 1986.

———. "Popular Culture in the Folklore Course." In *Popular Culture and Curricula*, Ray B. Browne and Ronald J. Ambrosetti, eds. Bowling Green, Ohio: Bowling Green Popular Press, 1972, pp. 61–72.

———. *The Study of American Folklore: An Introduction*. New York: Norton, 1968.

———. *The Vanishing Hitchhiker: American Urban Legends and Their Meanings*. New York: Norton, 1981.

Burnam, Tom. *More Misinformation*. New York: Lippincott and Crowell, 1980.

Campbell, Joseph. "Folkloristic Commentary." *The Complete Grimm's Fairy Tales*. 1944; repr. New York: Pantheon Books, 1972, pp. 833–864.

———. *The Masks of God: Primitive Mythology*. New York: Viking, 1970.

———. *The Mythic Image*. Princeton: Princeton University Press, 1974.

Carson, L. M. Kit. "'Saw' Thru." *Film Comment* 22 (1986): 10–11.

Carvalho-Neto, Paulo de. *Folklore and Psychoanalysis*. Jacques M. P. Wilson, trans. Coral Gables, Fla.: University of Miami Press, 1968.

Cerf, Bennet. "Trade Winds." *Saturday Review of Literature* 28 (1945): 16–17.

Ciment, Michel. *Kubrick*. Gilbert Adair, trans. New York: Holt, Rinehart, and Winston, 1983.

Clarens, Carlos. *Horror Movies: An Illustrated Survey*. London: Sacker and Warburg, 1968.

Clarke, Kenneth and Mary. *Introducing Folklore*. New York: Holt, Rinehart, and Winston, 1963.

Clouston, William Alexander. *Popular Tales and Fictions: Their Migrations and Transformations*. Detroit: Singing Tree Press, 1968.

Cocks, Jay. "Why He's a Thriller." *Time*, March 19, 1984, pp. 54–60.

Cohen, Barney. "Where B Means Brutal." *New York Times Magazine*, September 9, 1984, pp. 154–155, 165.

Cook, Elizabeth. *The Ordinary and the Fabulous: An Introduction to Myths, Legends, and Fairy Tales for Teachers and Storytellers*. Cambridge: Cambridge University Press, 1971.

Cott, Jonathan. *Pipers at the Gates of Dawn: The Wisdom of Children's Literature*. New York: Random House, 1983.

Crawford, Merritt. "Georges Méliès—The Jules Verne of the Cinema." *Cinema*, October 1930, pp. 27–30, 56.

Crawley, Tony. *The Steven Spielberg Story*. New York: Quill, 1983.

Dale, Rodney. *The Tumor in the Whale: A Collection of Modern Myths.* London: Duckworth, 1978.

Danielson, Larry. "Folklore and Film: Some Thoughts on Baughman Z 500–599." *Western Folklore* 38 (1979): 209–219.

Darnton, Robert. *The Great Cat Massacre and Other Episodes in French Cultural History.* New York: Basic Books, 1984.

Dégh, Linda. "The 'Belief Legend' in Modern Society: Form, Function, and Relationship to Other Genres." In *American Folk Legend*, Wayland D. Hand, ed. Berkeley: University of California Press, 1971, pp. 55–68.

———. *Folktales and Society: Story-Telling in a Hungarian Peasant Community.* Emily M. Schossberger, trans. Bloomington: Indiana University Press, 1969.

Dégh, Linda, and Andrew Vázsonyi. "The Dialectics of the Legend." *Folklore Reprint Series* 1, no. 6 (December 1973).

Denby, David, ed. *Awake in the Dark.* New York: Vintage Books, 1977.

DeVries, Leonard. *'Orrible Murder: Victorian Crime and Passion Compiled from the Illustrated Police News.* New York: Taplinger Publishing Co., 1971.

Dickson, Paul, and Joseph C. Goulden. *There Are Alligators in Our Sewers and Other American Credos.* New York: Delacorte Press, 1983.

Dickstein, Morris. "Peter Panavision." *In These Times* 7 (1983): 20–21, 24.

Dorson, Richard. *American Folklore.* Chicago: University of Chicago Press, 1959.

———. *Folklore: Selected Essays.* Bloomington: Indiana University Press, 1972.

———, ed. *Folklore and Folklife: An Introduction.* Chicago and London: University of Chicago Press, 1972.

Drake, Carlos C. "Jungian Psychology and Its Uses in Folklore." *Journal of American Folklore* 82 (1969): 122–131.

Dudley, Edward, and Maximilian E. Novak. *The Wild Man Within: An Image in Western Thought from the Renaissance to Romanticism.* Pittsburgh: University of Pittsburgh Press, 1972.

Dundes, Alan. "The Dead Baby Cycle." *Western Folklore* 3 (1979): 145–157.

———. "On the Psychology of Legend." In *American Folk Legend: A Symposium*, Wayland D. Hand, ed. Berkeley: University of California Press, 1971, pp. 21–36.

———. *The Study of Folklore.* Englewood Cliffs, N.J.: Prentice-Hall, 1965.

Eastman, Mary Huse. *Index to Fairy Tales, Myths, and Legends.* Boston: F. W. Faxon Co., 1926.

Eco, Umberto. *Travels in Hyperreality.* New York: Harcourt Brace Jovanovich, 1986.

Eisler, Benita. *Private Lives: Men and Women in the Fifties.* New York: Franklin Watts, 1986.

Eliade, Mircea. *Myth and Reality.* New York: Harper & Row, 1963.

———. *Myths, Dreams, and Mysteries.* New York: Harper & Row, 1975.

———. *Rites and Symbols of Initiation: The Mysteries of Death and Rebirth.* New York: Harper & Row, 1965.

Emrich, Duncan. *Folklore on the American Land.* Boston: Little, Brown, 1972.

Fell, John. *Film and the Narrative Tradition.* Norman, Okla.: University of Oklahoma Press, 1974.

Fiedler, Leslie. *Freaks: Myths and Images of the Secret Self.* New York: Simon and Schuster, 1978.

———. "Giving the Devil His Due." *Journal of Popular Culture* 12 (1979): 197–207.

———. *What Was Literature?: Class Culture and Mass Society.* New York: Simon and Schuster, 1982.

Fischer, J. L. "The Sociopsychological Analysis of Folktales." *Current Anthropology* 4 (1963): 235–295.

Flanagan, John T., and Arthur Palmer Hudson. *Folklore in American Literature.* New York: Harper & Row, 1958.

French, Warren. *J. D. Salinger.* New York: Twayne, 1963.

Freud, Sigmund. *Totem and Taboo.* Trans. James Strachey. New York: W. W. Norton, 1950.

Friedan, Betty. *The Feminine Mystique.* New York: W. W. Norton, 1963.

Friedman, Albert B. "The Usable Myth: The Legends of Modern Mythmakers." In *American Folk Legend: A Symposium*, Wayland D. Hand, ed. Berkeley: University of California Press, 1971, pp. 37–46.

Frye, Northrop. *Anatomy of Criticism: Four Essays.* Princeton: Princeton University Press, 1957.

———. "The Argument of Comedy." In *English Institute Essays, 1948*, D. A. Robertson, ed. New York: Columbia University Press, 1949, pp. 58–73.

Fussell, Paul. *Class: A Guide through the American Status System.* New York: Summit Books, 1983.

Gardner, Martin. "The Third Coming." *New York Review of Books,* January 26, 1978, pp. 21–22.

Gollmar, Robert. *Edward Gein.* New York: Pinnacle Books, 1984.

Gould, Stephen Jay. "Mickey Mouse Meets Konrad Lorenz." *Natural History* 88 (1979): 30–35.

Glicksohn, Susan Wood. *The Poison Maiden and the Great Bitch: Female Stereotypes in Marvel Superhero Comics.* Baltimore: T-K Graphics, 1974.

Greig, Francis. *Heads You Lose and Other Apocryphal Tales.* New York: Crown, 1982.

Grennan, Margaret R. "Lilliput and Leprecan: Gulliver and the Irish Tradition." *ELH* 12 (September 1945): 188–202.

Grotjahn, Martin. *Beyond Laughter.* New York: McGraw-Hill, 1957.

Gurko, Leo. *Heroes, Highbrows, and the Popular Mind.* Indianapolis and New York: Bobbs-Merrill, 1953.

Halpert, Herbert C., Bradford Mitchell, and David Dickson. "Folktales from Indiana University Students." *Hoosier Folklore Bulletin* 1 (1942): 85–97.

Hand, Wayland D., ed. *American Folk Legend: A Symposium.* Berkeley: University of California Press, 1971.

Harris, Marvin. *America Now: The Anthropology of a Changing Culture.* New York: Simon and Schuster, 1982.

Harris, Robert R. "Brand-Name Horror." *New York Times,* November 27, 1983, p. 43.

Hartland, Edwin Sidney. *English Fairy and Other Folk Tales.* London: Walter Scott, 1890.

———. "The Forbidden Chamber." *Folklore Journal* 3 (1885): 193–242.

Haughton, Rosemary. *Tales from Eternity: The World of Fairy Tales and the Spiritual Search.* New York: Seabury Press, 1973.

Hawthorne, Nathaniel. *The Celestial Railroad and Other Stories.* New York: Signet, 1963.

Hellerstein, David. "The Peter Pan Principle." *Esquire* 100 (October 1983): 64–74.

Heuscher, Julius E. *A Psychoanalytic Study of Fairy Tales: Their Origin, Meaning and Usefulness.* Springfield, Ill.: Charles C. Thomas, 1963.

Hillman, James. *Loose Ends: Primary Papers in Archetypal Psychology.* Zurich: Spring Publications, 1975.

———. "*Senex* and *Puer:* An Aspect of the Historical and Psychological Present." *Eranos-Jahrbuch 1967.* Zurich: Rhein Verlag, 1968, pp. 301–360.

Hirsch, Foster. "Fantastic Attractions." Review of *Omni's Screen Flights/Screen Fantasies. New York Times Book Review,* October 7, 1984, p. 16.

Hoberman, J., and Jonathan Rosenbaum. *Midnight Movies.* New York: Harper & Row, 1983.

Husband, Timothy. *The Wild Man: Medieval Myth and Symbol.* New York: The Metropolitan Museum of Art, 1980.

Jackson, Kenneth T. *Crabgrass Frontier: The Suburbanization of the United States.* New York and Oxford: Oxford University Press, 1985.

Jacobi, Jolande. *Complex/Archetype/Symbol.* Princeton: Princeton University Press, 1959.

Jacobs, Joseph. *English Fairy Tales.* 1898; repr. New York: Dover, 1967.

Jarrell, Mackie L. "'Jack and the Dane': Swift Tradition in Ireland." *Journal of American Folklore* 77 (1964): 99–117.

Johnson, Clifton. *What They Say in New England and Other American Folklore.* New York and London: Columbia University Press, 1963.

Jones, Ernest. "Psychoanalysis and Folklore." In *The Study of Folklore,* Alan Dundes, ed. Englewood Cliffs, N.J.: Prentice-Hall, 1965, pp. 88–102.

———. "The Symbolic Significance of Salt in Folklore and Superstition." *Essays in Applied Psychoanalysis, Vol 2: Essays on Folklore, Anthropology, and Religion.* London: The Hogarth Press, 1951, pp. 22–109.

Kaminsky, Stuart. *American Film Genres.* New York: Dell, 1974.

Keightley, Thomas. *The Fairy Mythology.* 1892; repr. London: Wildwood House, 1981.

Kelly, William. "More than a Woman: Myth and Mediation in *Saturday Night Fever.*" *Journal of American Culture* 2 (Summer 1979): 235–247.

King, Stephen. *Danse Macabre.* New York: Everest House, 1981.

———. *Night Shift.* New York: New American Library/Signet, 1979.

Kissel, Howard. "Peter Pan." *Horizon* 22 (1979): 17–24.

Kotzwinkle, William. *E.T., the Extraterrestrial.* New York: Berkley Books, 1982.

Kroll, Jack. "The UFO's Are Coming!" *Newsweek,* November 22, 1977, pp. 88–97.

La Barre, Weston. "Folklore and Psychology." *Journal of American Folklore* 61 (1948): 382–390.

Leach, MacEdward. "Folklore in American Regional Literature." *Journal of the Folklore Institute* 3 (1966): 376–397.

Legman, G. "Folk Literature and Folklore with a Few Words on Science Fiction." In *The Horn Book: Studies in Erotic Folklore.* New Hyde Park, N.Y.: University Books, 1964.

Loder, Kurt. "Night Creatures." *Rolling Stone,* August 2, 1984, pp. 118–121.

Lundquist, James. *J. D. Salinger.* New York: Frederick Ungar, 1979.

Lurie, Allison. *The Language of Clothes.* New York: Random House, 1981.

Luthi, Max. *Once upon a Time: On the Nature of Fairy Tales.* Bloomington, Ind.: Indiana University Press, 1976.

Lyons, Gene. "King of High-School Horror." *Newsweek,* May 7, 1983, p. 76.

MacDougall, Curtis D. *Superstition and the Press.* Buffalo, N.Y.: Prometheus Books, 1983.

McCarthy, Todd, and Charles Flynn. *Kings of the B's: Working within the Hollywood System.* New York: E. P. Dutton, 1975.

McCarty, John. *Splatter Movies.* New York: St. Martin's Press, 1984.

McLuhan, Marshall. *The Mechanical Bride: Folklore of Industrial Man.* New York: The Vanguard Press, 1951.

Martin, Ralph G. "A New Life Style." In *Suburbia in Transition,* Louis H. Masotti and Jeffrey K. Haddon, eds. New York: Franklin Watts/New Viewpoints, 1974, pp. 14–21.

Maslin, Janet. "Hippie Nostalgia." *New York Times,* November 23, 1983, section C, p. 16.

Matheson, Richard. *The Incredible Shrinking Man.* London: Corgi Books, 1983.

Medved, Harry and Michael. *Son of Golden Turkey Awards.* New York: Random House/Villard Books, 1986.

Melville, Herman. *Typee: A Peep at Polynesian Life.* Evanston and Chicago: Northwestern-Newberry, 1968.

Moellenhoff, F. "Remarks on the Popularity of Mickey Mouse." *American Imago* 1 (1940): 19–32.

Muller, Peter O. *Contemporary Suburban America.* Englewood Cliffs, N.J.: Prentice-Hall, 1981.

Nelson, Bryce. "The Alien Already Here: Insights into E.T.'s Power." *New York Times,* December 21, 1982, section C, p. 14.

Nelson, Thomas Allen. *Kubrick: Inside a Film Artist's Maze.* Bloomington: Indiana University Press, 1982.

Opie, Iona and Peter. *The Classic Fairy Tales.* London: Oxford University Press, 1974.

Panofsky, Erwin. "Style and Medium in the Motion Pictures." In *Awake in the Dark,* David Denby, ed. New York: Vintage Books, 1977, pp. 30–48.

Partridge, J. B. "Notes on English Folklore." *Folklore* 28 (1917): 311–315.

Prawer, S. S. *Caligari's Children: The Film as Tale of Terror.* Oxford: Oxford University Press, 1980.

Prose, Francine. *Bigfoot Dreams.* New York: Pantheon, 1986.

Raitt, Jill. "The *Vagina Dentata* and the *Immaculatus Uterus Divini Fontis.*" *Journal of the American Academy of Religion* 48 (1950): 415–431.

Reaver, J. Russell. "'Embalmed Alive': A Developing Urban Ghost Tale." *New York Folklore Quarterly* 8 (1952): 217–220.

Righter, William. *Myth and Literature.* London: Routledge & Kegan Paul, 1975.

Robertson, D. A., ed. *English Institute Essays, 1948.* New York: Columbia University Press, 1949.

Roszak, Theodore. *The Making of a Counter Culture: Reflections on the Technocratic Society and Its Youthful Opposition.* Garden City, N.Y.: Doubleday/Anchor, 1969.

Russell, W. M. S. "Folktales and Science Fiction." *Folklore* 93 (1982): 3–30.

Salinger, J. D. "A Boy in France." *Saturday Evening Post,* March 31, 1945, pp. 21, 92.

———. "The Last Day of the Last Furlough." *Saturday Evening Post,* July 15, 1944, pp. 26–27, 61–62, 64.

———. "This Sandwich Has No Mayonnaise." *Esquire* 24 (1945): pp. 54–56, 147–149.

———. "The Stranger." *Colliers,* December 1, 1945, pp. 18, 77.

Schreiner, David. "Ed Gein and the Left Hand of God." *Weird Trips* 2 (1978): 20–32.

Schroeder, Fred E. H. "*National Enquirer* Is National Fetish! The Untold Story!" In *Objects of Special Devotion: Fetishes and Fetishism in Popular Culture*, Ray B. Browne, ed. Bowling Green, Ohio: Bowling Green University Popular Press, 1982, pp. 168–181.

Short, Robert. *The Gospel from Outer Space*. New York: Harper & Row, 1983.

Simpson, Jacqueline. "Rationalized Motifs in Urban Legends." *Folklore* 92 (1981): 203–207.

Singer, Jerome L. *Daydreaming and Fantasy*. London: George Allen & Unwin, Ltd., 1976.

Skinner, Charles M. *Myths and Legends of Our Own Land*. Philadelphia: J. B. Lippincott, 1896.

Smith, Marion W. "Musings on Folklore, 1943." *Journal of American Folklore* 57 (1946): 70–72.

Solensten, John M. "Hawthorne's Ribald Classic: 'Mrs. Bullfrog' and the Folktale." *Journal of Popular Culture* 7 (1973): 582–588.

Stashower, Daniel M. "On First Looking into Chapman's Holden." *American Scholar* 52 (Summer 1983): 373–377.

Steel, Flora Annie. *English Fairy Tales*. New York: Macmillan, 1918.

Steranko, Jim. *History of Comics—Volume One*. Reading, Pa.: Supergraphics, 1970.

Stone, Kay. "Things Walt Disney Never Told Us." *Journal of American Folklore* 88 (1975): 42–50.

Strecker, John K. "Reptiles of the South and Southwest in Folklore." *Publications of the Texas Folklore Society* 5 (1926): 56–69.

Taylor, Archer. "Folklore and the Student of Literature." In *The Study of Folklore*, Alan Dundes, ed. Englewood Cliffs, N.J.: Prentice-Hall, 1965.

Thompson, David. "Sex in Science Fiction Films: Romance or Engineering?" In *Omni's Screen Flights/Screen Fantasies*, Danny Peary, ed. New York: Doubleday, 1984, pp. 56–66.

Thompson, Harold W. *Body, Boots & Britches: Folktales, Ballads and Speech from County New York*. New York: J. B. Lippincott, 1939.

Thompson, Stith. *Motif-Index of Folk Literature*. Bloomington: Indiana University Press, 1955–1958.

———. *The Folktale*. New York: Holt, Rinehart and Winston, 1946.

Thurber, James. *Alarms & Diversions*. New York: Harper & Row/ Perennial Library, 1964.

Toelken, Barre. *The Dynamics of Folklore*. Boston: Houghton Mifflin, 1979.

Tolkien, J. R. R. *Tree and Leaf.* Boston: Houghton Mifflin, 1965.

Train, John. *True Remarkable Occurrences.* New York: Clarkson Potter, 1978.

Twitchell, James B. *Dreadful Pleasures: An Anatomy of Modern Horror.* New York: Oxford University Press, 1985.

Updike, John. *Hugging the Shore.* New York: Knopf, 1983.

Ussher, Arland, and Carl von Metzradt. *Enter These Enchanted Woods: An Interpretation of Grimm's Fairy Tales.* Dublin: The Dolman Press, 1957.

Von Franz, Marie-Louise. *An Introduction to the Interpretation of Fairy Tales.* New York: Sprint Publications, 1970.

———. *Puer Aeternus.* Santa Monica, Calif.: Sigo Press, 1981.

Wahlstrom, Billie, and Caren Deming. "Chasing the Popular Arts through the Critical Forest." *Journal of Popular Culture* 13 (1980): 412–426.

Warshow, Robert. *The Immediate Experience: Movies, Comics, Theatre and Other Aspects of Popular Culture.* Garden City, N.Y.: Doubleday, 1962.

Waters, John. "Why I Love the *National Enquirer.*" *Rolling Stone*, October 10, 1985, pp. 43–44, 71.

Weigle, Marta. *Spiders & Spinsters: Women and Mythology.* Albuquerque: University of New Mexico Press, 1982.

White, Beatrice. "A Persistent Paradox." *Folklore* 83 (1972): 122–131.

Whitmont, Edward C. *The Symbolic Quest.* New York: Harper & Row, 1969.

Wood, Robin. "Return of the Repressed." *Film Comment* 14 (1978): 26.

Wright, A. R. "Animals in People's Insides." *Folk-Lore* 41 (1930): 105–106.

Yearsley, MacLeod. *The Folklore of Fairy-Tale.* 1924; repr. Detroit, Mich. Singing Tree Press, 1968.

Zipes, Jack. *Fairy Tales and the Art of Subversion: The Classical Genre for Civilization and the Process of Civilization.* New York: Wildman Press, 1983.

Index